THE
BREAD
BOOK

A Natural, Whole-Grain Seed-to-Loaf Approach to Real Bread

By Thom Leonard

FOREWORD BY LAUREL ROBERTSON

D1282630

EAST WEST HEALTH BOOKS
1990

EAST WEST HEALTH BOOKS
17 Station Street
Brookline, Massachusetts 02146

ISBN 0-936184-09-4

Published in the United States of America

First Edition

135798642

Distributed to the natural foods trade by
East West Health Books, 17 Station Street, Brookline, MA 02146
and to the book trade by
The Talman Company, 150 Fifth Avenue, New York, NY 10011

Cover and text design by Betsy Woldman
Cover and text photos by Ed Slaman

Also from East West Health Books:

Meetings with Remarkable Men and Women

Natural Childcare

Cooking with Japanese Foods

Sweet & Natural Desserts

TABLE OF CONTENTS

ACKNOWLEDGMENTS

Most of the material in this book first appeared as articles in the pages of *East West: The Journal of Natural Health and Living*. Through the years the publisher and my friend, Leonard Jacobs, has given me much support and encouragement. Editors Mark Mayell, Linda Elliot, and Meg Seaker have kept my style in line and have not allowed me to go more than a year past deadline. Managing Editor Dan Seamens has had the thankless task of keeping me working on this book when I'd rather be sowing wheat or building a new oven.

Derbhail Ryan co-authored the original version of the pizza chapter and most of the delectable recipes are hers. Alan Scott supplied the inspiration, plans, and actual instructions for oven building. Bjorn and Gunda Lunde let me (and helped) build an oven in their backyard. Laurel Robertson repeatedly reminded me that this book was special enough to write.

Jane McClendon first guided my hands to dough. Her sister, Jeannie Orr, nurtured the growing practice at The Bakery in Point Arena, California. Hy Lerner of Baldwin Hill Bakery in Phillipston, Mass., gave new meaning to bread and taught me to make the real thing and to accept no substitutes.

These people and others too numerous to mention have all influenced my bread making and the content of this book. Their influence is obvious to me and likely will be to them if they read this book. I am grateful to them and give them credit for all my successes and for yours that will follow. For all that isn't clear, and for all the loaves that never rise, I take full responsibility.

Thom Leonard
Salina, Kansas
January 1990

FOREWORD

A few years back, when friends and I were writing a book about whole-grain bread, a puckish neighbor persuaded us that we wouldn't really know "all about wheat" until we had raised our own. He even offered a twice-tilled half acre. How could we resist?

We chose a bag of the wheat berries we liked best for bread, and one moonlit evening three of us marched out and flung grain all over the place. In the morning the field was carpeted with ecstatic blackbirds. They must have missed a lot, though, because the wheat came up anyway, tender and then lush.

The greenness was overwhelming—sweet-smelling and breathtakingly beautiful. By mid-August the field had turned to burnished gold. It was thrilling. What started on a dare was now something we pointed out with pride. "Yes, that's our wheat patch. Isn't it fantastic?"

Bright gold turned to tan, and thunderheads glowered on the northern hills. The time had come! Armed with a couple of rusty sickles from the landlord's shed, we headed for the field on the hottest day in fifty years. After a few hours a new consensus emerged: It's been a great experiment, and the blackbirds are so happy, let's call it a day. I think it was Helen who stuck it out long enough to make a double row of makeshift shocks to stand picturesquely along the top edge of the field.

How do you get the wheat away from the straw? (Well? How do you?) Beating it with sticks and throwing it into the windless air produced plenty of hilarity but not much usable grain. In the end we had enough to make flour for one loaf of bread—one *delicious* loaf. We shared it with awe and a silent agreement that (as my father would say) this was a great experience to have behind you.

A couple of years later, twinkle in eyes, Helen showed me an article in *East West* by Thom Leonard titled "The Bread Patch." I couldn't believe it. Come on! Are they actually telling people to grow their own wheat? But, well, Thom's stuff's always worth reading. . . . Lo and behold, he had practical solutions to every problem we had hit along our wheatpatching way, even the straw!

That's the way it is in all of Thom's articles, from oven building to baking airy unyeasted bread. And his comparisons of various grain mills are the best and most helpful I've seen. I must have sent dozens of people to the library to consult them in *East West*'s back issues.

Thom is an uncommonly good writer, but he's a *real* farmer and baker; everything he says comes from living and doing. His dedication—and a fine whimsy—lights every page. The things he writes about are basic, real, and essential. His magic lies in his ability to make us see that doing them is not too hard and neither silly nor far-fetched, but a source of joy day to day.

I think, maybe, we will try wheat again. And a little barley too— the brown hull-less kind that makes such good breakfast cereal.

Laurel Robertson
Petaluma, California
January 1990

INTRODUCTION

Another bread book? Yes, but I think unlike any other that you've seen. The breads you'll make from this book are all naturally leavened, made without baker's yeast or chemical rising agents. And what other bread book tells you tales of old water-powered grain mills in Ireland, helps you choose a home mill, walks you through the process of building your own wood-fired brick oven, and shows you how to grow a patch of wheat in your own backyard?

"But I don't want to grow wheat," you may say to yourself. "Build a brick oven in my fourth floor walk-up? Right. And I'll scavenge the streets of the pre-trash-pick-up dawn for discarded shipping pallets to fire it." Fear not. All of the recipes in this book were written for and tested with store-bought wheat and cooked to perfection in standard home gas and electric range ovens. But do build a brick oven if you possibly can. You will be able to tell the difference; not only in the rise, the crust, and the taste of the loaf, but also in the quality of your baking day, and in the new life that the oven will bring to your home.

The first bread I baked some twenty years ago was made with flour we had ground in a hand-cranked Corona mill only minutes before mixing the dough. And most of the bread I have made since has been made with freshly milled flour. Ignore what commercial millers and bakers tell you about how aging improves flour. Whole-grain flours and meals begin to deteriorate almost as soon as they are ground. The flavor of a naturally leavened loaf made with freshly ground whole wheat flour is incomparable. It tastes like—of all things—wheat. If good bread is important to you, either get a household mill or shop at a store that guarantees fresh flour.

Naturally leavened bread is bread that has been fermented and risen with a mixed culture of naturally occurring microorganisms that is saved and passed on from batch to batch. This culture helps create a special loaf that takes a bit of extra work to produce. But after the initial preparation of your leaven culture, which you may do only once in your lifetime, it really is not that much more work than making bread with commercial yeast.

What's so special about bread made with natural leavening? Author and natural foods authority Ron Kotzsch put the value of a naturally leavened loaf into proper perspective when he wrote:

> Let's suppose we want to bake a loaf of real "traditional" bread, the same as nourished our European ancestors. We gather the simplest and best ingredients: whole-grain wheat and rye, pure water, sea salt, and the finest cake yeast available. We grind the grain into flour. We start the yeast in warm water, then blend that frothy mix with flour, making a dough. Dressed in medieval peasant garb and reciting our favorite Chaucerian bawdy verse, we knead the dough, let it rise and knead it again. After allowing a final proofing, or rise, in baking pans, we bake it slowly in a wood-fired brick oven. The bread emerges golden brown, filling the house with its earthy and sweet aroma. Our ancestors smile benignly down from their celestial (we hope) posts, fluttering angelic wings in approval. We have faithfully recreated the staff of life, the nutritional cornerstone of Western civilization for centuries.
>
> Right? Wrong! Despite our consummate care, we have not made traditional bread at all. Rather, we have produced something which, until the late 19th century, was completely unknown, which for years afterwards was banned by the French government, and which has been linked by modern researchers to anemia, rickets, intestinal problems, even cancer. We have made only one error, but it is a crucial one. We have used the wrong leavening agent: baker's yeast.

I might push Kotzsch's argument a little further. I question whether that what we make when we use baker's yeast instead of natural leavening can be called bread at all.

Many naturally leavened breads have survived well into this century. Some of these—San Francisco sourdough, European sour rye, and "Parisian barm" (oddly, natural leavening widely used in Scotland around the turn of the century)—have been carefully studied. They each exhibit, in addition to one or more yeasts, at least one and often several species of lactic acid bacteria. The different organisms cooperate in creating a favorable environment for one another. Together they create conditions that suppress the development of populations of organisms that would weaken the culture.

Traditional bread leavening, like virtually all traditional

fermented foods, is in effect a living ecosystem—multi-specied, complex, more like a forest or the native prairie than like a pulpwood plantation or an Iowa cornfield. No one even tries to suggest that a field of mono-cropped corn is a tallgrass prairie ecosystem. And if a cornfield is not a prairie, how can a dough seeded with one purified variety of yeast be called bread?

When I first began baking, I envisioned the conditions necessary for creating the perfect loaf: freshly ground flour of organically grown wheat, sourdough natural leavening, pure water, and a wood-fired brick oven. It was my goal to be part of a bakery that met all of these conditions. That honor was mine in the early 1980s when I worked with Hy Lerner at his incomparable Baldwin Hill Bakery in rural Massachusetts. But standards and goals change. I now feel that the joys of natural baking should not be reserved for professional bakers. The best bread is that which can be made at home and with locally grown grain of a traditional variety.

Today I bake virtually all of my bread with Turkey Red, a hard red winter wheat, mostly harvested from patches and fields that I tend with friends here in Saline County, Kansas. Turkey wheat was brought to Kansas from Crimea by Mennonite immigrants in the early 1870s. While Turkey has been important in the breeding of virtually all the hard red wheat grown in the central plains, it is no longer grown on farms. The wheats that have replaced it may yield higher and may have resistance to a few more diseases than Turkey, but they cannot surpass it in flavor, nor in longevity. In twenty years many of these new wheats will be forgotten. Turkey will persist for those few of us who value tradition, resilience, and taste.

Turkey is but one of countless varieties of traditional grains endangered (or already extinct) because of the practices of modern agribusiness. If we seek out the traditional varieties that remain, grow them or have them grown, and use them to prepare our favorite foods, we will have at least done something to preserve some of the rich diversity that our ancestors have given to us. But, just as you don't need a wood-fired brick oven to bake bread, nor do you need a traditional wheat to produce a naturally leavened loaf. I do, however, heartily recommend that you use the best salt you can find, pure water, and flour milled from organically grown grains. Mostly, I hope you enjoy this book and have many perfect loaves for many wonderful meals. Happy baking.

Thom Leonard
Salina, Kansas
January 1990

THE BREAD PATCH

UNTIL THE OPENING OF THE NORTH AMERICAN PLAINS IN THE EARLY NINETEENTH CENTURY, GRAIN WAS GROWN MOSTLY IN PATCHES, a little in fields, and not at all in landscape-size panoramic plantings. And until Cyrus McCormick invented his reaper in 1834, all grain was harvested by human labor with simple hand tools. In many places in the world these practices survive to this day. But for we who dwell in the industrialized world, grain growing, once a skill practiced by many, has become a business practiced by few. And those few wield 150-horsepower tractors and combines that cut superhighway-wide swaths through seas of golden grain.

The patch-grown grain of centuries past provided first the bread for the family. Any surplus was sold on the market or given to the village miller in trade for his services. Today precious few Kansas wheat farmers eat the bread of their own fields. Most eat store-bought sliced white sandwich bread baked in Hutchinson or Dodge City, made from flour milled in Kansas City from a blend of wheats, some grown as far away as Montana. And these wheats are all from modern varieties selected for high yield, uniformity of growth characteristics, and response to chemical inputs. A farm family actually gets a lower price for their wheat if they bring in a load of Turkey Red, the grandfather of all the Kansas wheats. They'll be docked because this venerable Old World wheat lacks what is today considered "good milling and baking qualities."

By growing small plots of wheat and other small grains (as

1

opposed to large grains such as corn) in your backyard vegetable garden, you can begin to restore the practice of "growing bread," uniting yourself with subsistence farmers past and present around the globe, and perhaps save an heirloom grain strain and an ancient art as well.

I remember the mornings in late spring of the first year I planted rye in the backyard. The silvery blue-green stalks with ears as high as my own blew gently in the breezes, undulating like a pond of green waves. The heads formed, with long, spike-like awns, and the grain swelled. Soon the long and slender ears, bowed with the weight of the grain, arched, and the dew-jeweled rye became ten thousand marlin leaping from a blue-green sea. There is an incomparable magic, a peace, a stillness in standing among these plants, one that farmers have known for thousands of years.

It's easy to grow grain. It's also surprising how much can be harvested from a carefully tended small plot. Ecology Action, a research and educational center in Willits, California, projects yields as high as twenty-six pounds per 100 square feet with their "biointensive" raised-bed method. If such a yield were achieved from one four-foot-wide garden bed twenty-five feet long, enough wheat could be harvested to make twenty-five one and three-quarter pound loaves of bread, with a lot less work than you'd put into the same bed planted to vegetables. A Kansas wheat farmer is likely to get five pounds of wheat from the same area in a field. In order to get such high yields you must have a high level of organic matter in your soil, be growing in the loose soil of a raised bed, and be able to water in dry periods. Somewhat lower yields can be had with less intensive practices, but you'd have a hard time not getting eight or ten pounds in one hundred square feet of good garden soil supplied with adequate moisture. That's still ten large loaves of bread. And you get more than the grain itself. The roots of a single rye plant can grow a combined three miles in one day and as much as 380 miles in a season. That "root manure" remains in the soil as unseen organic matter. The straw from whatever grain you grow returns to the garden as mulch or compost, and if you overseed with clover (more on this later), you get another crop that goes entirely to enrich the soil.

CHOOSING YOUR GRAIN

The primary bread grains, wheat and rye, are the easiest of the small grains to grow and prepare to eat. There are varieties of wheat adapted to spring planting and others to fall planting, known respectively as spring and winter wheat. Spring wheat is generally grown in areas with extremely cold winters, mostly the northern plains, where winter wheat is prone to winterkill—damage from the extreme temperatures.

There are advantages to both types. Winter wheat will give a higher yield, keep the ground covered over the winter, and will have little trouble competing with weeds. Winter wheat is usually grown anywhere it can survive the winter. It can be planted in an area of the garden that won't be harvested until late fall (which would be too late for planting winter wheat). Spring wheat will generally contain more protein than a similar type of winter wheat. Perhaps most important, it makes growing wheat possible in areas with severe winters.

The best way to know whether to plant winter or spring wheat is to ask your county agricultural extension agent or a local farmer. Unless you live in the extreme north of the United States, winter wheat should pose no problem. On the other hand, if spring planting fits your garden plan better, and you don't mind the lower yields, spring wheat can be grown farther south than it is commercially planted. Be sure to get it in as early as the soil can be worked—perhaps prepare an area in the fall before snowfall—and be prepared for competition from more weeds than with winter wheat.

Besides choosing between winter and spring wheat, you also need to decide whether to grow hard or soft, red or white wheat. Hard wheats have more protein and are generally considered better for bread making, but they are adapted for the growing and soil conditions of the drier high plains, and won't do well in the damp eastern part of the U.S. The Pacific Rim of North America, with its varying climatic conditions due to the interaction of several mountain ranges and the Pacific Ocean, has areas suited to both hard and soft wheat. In damp climates sow soft wheat. Grown in areas with high rainfall, hard wheats are nearly as soft and as low in protein as soft varieties and don't grow or yield as well. My experience has been that a well-grown, properly milled soft wheat will make better bread than a hard wheat grown out of place. Soft wheat is ideal for pastries, cookies, and crackers, and although most American and European pasta is made from the very hard durum wheat, the Japanese wheat pastas *udon* and *somen* are made from soft white wheat. Again, check with your extension agent to find out what's best for your area.

Although hard white bread wheat was once grown, virtually all hard wheat grown in the U.S. today is red. Soft white wheat is grown in the Pacific Northwest and on a smaller scale in the Great Lakes Region and New York State. If you want a light-colored, soft whole wheat flour, plant a white variety if you can find it. Red wheat, both hard and soft, is much more common.

Winter wheat is planted, depending on location and weather conditions, from mid-September to late October. One year I got a good stand in my northwest Arkansas garden from a crop planted just before Thanksgiving. But I was lucky that we had a late winter that year. To avoid the wheat pest Hessian fly, be sure to plant after the "fly-free date" for your area (once again, call your extension office). Get the seed into the ground long enough before winter sets in so that the wheat has time to develop a good root system before the cold sends it into dormancy.

Once you've decided whether to grow winter or spring, hard or soft, red or white wheat, there's another choice: what variety to plant. Just as there are many varieties of leaf lettuce, there are dozens of possible choices for, say, a soft red winter wheat. Most modern strains don't vary much from one another, and there are so many named and numbered varieties from different seed companies that it's impossible to recommend any particular one. Here are a few general considerations, though, to keep in mind.

Getting grain seed in small quantities can be a problem. Only a few catalogs offer it in garden-size packets. Mostly it's sold by the bushel—about sixty pounds. Because most wheat seed is treated with a fungicide, if you are able to buy a pound or two from a seed company try to obtain untreated seed. The treatment is not good for you, soil microorganisms, or the birds that will undoubtedly eat some of your seed. If all else fails, your local natural foods store bins can serve as a source of reasonably priced grain seed. And you'll solve the problem of deciding what variety to plant—you won't have a choice. The variety you get may not be ideally suited to your conditions, but it will grow and yield a good crop of grain. Just be sure not to plant a spring wheat variety in the fall or a winter wheat in the spring. By planting time next year, you should be able to track down a better source of seed.

SOWING GOOD SEED

Wheat should be grown on reasonably good soil, ideally enriched with a good, balanced, mature compost. If too much nitrogen is provided for the crop the stalks will "lodge" or fall over in the spring when the grain sets. Adequate phosphorus from rock phosphate will help the wheat plants to develop stronger stems and resist lodging.

There are a number of basic patterns suited to the sowing of bread grains. The simplest of these is to scatter—broadcast—the seed over a prepared seedbed and rake to cover the seed. Try for approximately one seed per square inch. This approach is best for large areas, but can also be used for planting raised beds, though "sprinkling" more accurately describes how you'd scatter seed on a four-foot-wide bed. Instead of raking the surface to cover the seed, a light covering of straw mulch scattered over the planted area can be substituted. In order to germinate and grow, the seed needs moisture, contact with the soil, and protection from hungry birds. Either raking or mulching provide all of this.

Another sowing approach is to sow in drills. That is, to make shallow furrows six or seven inches apart and plant a seed every inch or two. Broadcasting does have the distinct advantage of being a lot less work at planting time, but drills can be cultivated with a hoe to keep down weeds and to conserve soil moisture. If you'll be harvesting with a hand-held sickle, the work will go easier if the grain is planted in rows. But with fall-sown wheat there's little chance of weeds being a problem, especially if you've kept weeds down in the garden for a few seasons.

In his 1911 classic on permanent agriculture in the Far East, *Farmers of Forty Centuries*, F. H. King noted that Chinese farmers in Shantung and Tsinan provinces harvested respectable crops in a drought year and had excellent yields—even by today's standards—in years with normal rainfall. Here the wheat was "always planted in rows. . .hoed and in astonishingly good condition." The rows were in pairs, with sixteen inches between the rows in each pair and thirty inches between pairs. King detailed several advantages to this approach. It facilitated frequent hoeing, which helped to conserve moisture by maintaining a dust mulch. It made it possible to fertilize the plants when they could "use the food to best advantage" and to repeat feedings if necessary. Finally, the space between the pairs could be "fitted, fertilized, and another crop planted before the first is removed." In a year with normal rainfall these Chinese "patch farmers" harvested over 118 bushels to the acre, more than three times the *current* U.S. national average. During the same year they harvested, from the same land, a crop of cotton and one of greens as well. We can have yields like this in our intensive gardens; farmers tending extensive plantings of grain can only dream about them.

If you decide to plant in drills—either in raised beds or on the flat—make furrows two or three inches deep and sow the seed thinly (one seed every inch or two). Cover, and firm the earth over the row. If you plan to have more than a small patch, you'll probably want to get a small wheel-type garden seeder. In one pass, it will make the furrow, drop the seed, cover it, and mark the next row. With this simple tool, you could sow in short order a patch big enough to provide all your family's bread for a year. Expect to use two ounces of seed per 100 square feet for drilled wheat, three for broadcast.

WAITING FOR YOUR AMBER WAVES

The seed's in the ground, it's early October—what's next? Within a week small green shoots will show through the soil. The grain will continue to grow until cold weather sets in, establishing a strong root system. If winter is late in coming or fall is especially warm (always the case in the South), it might be good to clip the wheat once to prevent it from "stooling" or sending up a stalk—all you want is blades of grass before winter comes. Wheat farmers will often let cattle graze their winter wheat fields. Plants that have stooled are more susceptible to winterkill. You probably don't have a steer to turn loose in the backyard, but cutting with a lawn mower set on high or a sickle will serve the same purpose. The clippings can be left where they fall or raked up to feed the compost pile or your rabbits. In the northern half of the country this clipping won't be needed except in unusually warm years.

Mostly what you do now is wait until harvest in June or July. If you can afford to have the bread patch out of vegetable production for the entire next growing season, you might want to do what many Midwestern farmers do and "overseed" a leguminous cover crop into the wheat. This is usually done in late winter, before the wheat begins to grow again. The seed will germinate and begin to grow in the shadow of the wheat as the weather turns warm. After the grain is harvested, more sun gets to the cover and it takes over, providing a verdant blanket for the soil and nitrogen for the next crop. If you have a good stand, you can cut it once during the summer, let the "hay" cure for a day or two in the sun, rake it, and use it for compost, mulch, or feed. A low-growing white clover, such as white Dutch clover, is a good choice for this. Two ounces is more than enough for one twenty-five-by-four-foot bed or every hundred square feet of your larger bread patch.

There's one other thing you might want to do, especially if your soil is not very rich. When the wheat begins to grow in the spring, "top-dress" with manure or compost. Just sprinkle a little crumbly aged manure or compost over the patch. If your soil is well supplied with organic matter this shouldn't be necessary.

Most other grain crops are grown very much like wheat. Rye can be grown exactly like winter wheat, though it is hardier, can be planted later, and thrives on poorer soil. Some varieties grow to over five feet high. There are both winter and spring barleys. Oats, a spring sown crop in the North, is fall sown in the South. Millet is spring or summer sown, requires little rainfall, and some varieties mature in a very short period. Buckwheat (not a true grain) can be planted any time during the growing season, up to within sixty days of the first killing frost. It is very fast growing and smothers weeds—no need to plant in rows for ease of cultivating.

The trouble with growing buckwheat, millet, oats, and barley in the garden is the subsequent difficulty in using them in the kitchen. Wheat and rye "thresh clean," free of their glumes (outer husks) and hulls. Not so for most common varieties of these other grains. Unhulled buckwheat can be milled into flour and sifted to remove the hulls, but that's no good if you want kasha and not buckwheat flapjacks. As for oats, millet, and barley, I know of no simple way to remove their tenacious hulls on a home scale. Hull-less oats are available from at least one seed company. Hull-less barley, though relatively common in Asia, is available to gardeners only through seed exchanges in the United States.

Can grains be grown continuously on the same plot of ground without cultivation and without depleting the soil? Natural farming pioneer and *The One-Straw Revolution* author Masanobu Fukuoka has done so with remarkable success with rice and barley in Japan. To my knowledge, no one has yet adapted Fukuoka's approach to growing grains without rice in the system. Rice is important because flooding after seeding inhibits weed and clover growth and encourages rice growth. Other cereals do not thrive in water.

How can weed and clover growth be held in check without also inhibiting the growth of the crop? The garden bread patch is one place to look for answers. With rye it should work. Rye grows fast and tall. Short clover will not interfere with the harvest of the grain heads. Two conditions have to be met: 1) the rye has to germinate and take hold in the fall when the clover is still growing; and 2) the clover must be slower to start growing in the spring than the rye. I've been unable to find a leguminous perennial that remains dormant until the weather warms to above 40° to 45°F when rye starts its growth.

So that's all there is to it. Basically, prepare the soil, sow the seed, and wait until harvest. By late spring you should have a tiny green sea of waving grain. As summer approaches and it turns to gold in the sun you can prepare to harvest your first crop of bread.

For those of you who would like to grow a primitive wheat, and do your own small bit to keep an old strain alive, Redwood City Seed Company will, crops willing, offer several varieties of primitive grains. If you'd like a listing of what's available, send a SASE early in the spring to:

Redwood City Seed Company
Box 361
Redwood City, CA 94064
(regular catalog $1.00)

Peace Seeds offers a hull-less buckwheat and many other interesting items.
Peace Seeds
2385 SE Thompson St.
Corvallis, OR 97333

The KUSA Research Foundation offers an ancient millet variety, Dragon's Claw, at 350 seeds for $1.50.
KUSA Research Foundation
Box 761
Ojai, CA 93023

The following seed companies offer garden-size quantities of wheat, rye, buckwheat, or clover. Others probably do too.
Johnny's Selected Seeds
Albion, ME 05910
(catalog free)

Bountiful Gardens
Ecology Action
5798 Ridgewood Road
Willits, CA 95490

Some members of Seed Savers Exchange offer/seek heirloom grains. For information, send SASE to:
Seed Savers Exchange
RR 3, Box 239
Decorah, IA 52101
(membership $15.00)

The Grain Exchange offers a variety of grains suitable for garden-sized patches.
The Grain Exchange
Garden Grains
2440 East Water Well Road
Salina, KS 67401
(catalog $1.00)

BRINGING IN THE SHEAVES

T
HERE IS LITTLE IN MODERN AGRICULTURE TO
COMPARE WITH THE EXQUISITE BEAUTY OF A
FIELD OF CAREFUL WHEAT SHOCKS SEEN
through the early mist of a summer morning—especially if you were
binding and shocking until sundown the day before. In his 1917
treatise, *Equipment for the Farm and Farmstead*, Harry C. Ramsower
wrote, "Within the memory of men still living, the cradle, and even
the sickle, has been replaced by the modern four-horse, eight-foot-cut
grain-binder now used in almost every country in the world where
wheat is grown."

Where before men and women would cut the fields of grain with
hand tools, bind the cut wheat into sheaves, stack them into shocks,
and later thresh and winnow the grain, the laborious work of reaping
and binding was by Ramsower's time nearly completely taken over by
a machine powered by horses. With the subsequent introduction of
the combined reaper-thresher, now simply called a "combine," the
threshing itself was performed at harvest in the field by the same
machine that cut (reaped) the grain. Shocks of wheat standing in pre-
cision rows in fields of golden wheat stubble have become largely a
memory of our agrarian past.

While I don't expect to see agribusiness forsaking its efficiency in
the name of beauty, we bread-patch grain growers can. Indeed, it is
no sacrifice; the old ways are much more practical on our mini-farms
and gardens than modern machine-harvesters would be. Just as we
can save the genetic heritage of older cereal varieties by growing them

in our food gardens, so, too, can we preserve a cultural heritage—the magic and beauty of the harvest—in order that our children's children may know more of the old ways than what is gleaned from photographs, paintings, and writings of a distant past.

By early June your grain crop should be ripening if you live in a southern area and heading out if you live farther north. More northerly yet and probably your spring-sown crop is now knee high. So what next, well may you ask. How do I get this grass to turn into bread? Well, first, wait. Wait until the stalks turn yellow, with just a few streaks of green. Wait until the heads begin to bow, signaling the end of their heavenward growth and their return to the earth. Wait for a warm and sunny day, but don't wait until the seed is dead ripe, hard, and crunchy, and the stalks a uniform golden or yellow. Combine harvesters cut their fields at this stage, but farmers of old, like good bread-patch farmers, let their grain finish maturing in the shock. When you cut your grain, the kernels should be in the "soft dough" stage: no longer soft and milky, and not yet hard and dry, but halfway between. Of course, if you have planted a large patch of grain, and have access to a combine, do wait until the grain is ripe, since uncured grain never reaches true maturity and full ripeness if threshed from the heads. And the moisture content may be too high for safe storage without further drying. But more on that later. For now let's assume that you have a small patch of grain reaching maturity in your garden. What tools are needed to get your crop in?

HAND TOOLS

First, you will need something with which to cut the grain stalks. For a small patch, say only one garden bed, a sharp kitchen knife, a pair of shears, or pruners will suffice. On larger patches, I have used various types of sickles, scythes, and a grain cradle. Of these the scythe, a nearly perfect tool for mowing grass and hay, is the least suited to the task. The severed stalks are left in disarray, and must be gathered and straightened out to make sheaves. A cradle, basically just a scythe with a "cradle" to catch the cut grain, can work beautifully on larger plantings if the reaper is skilled and careful, leaving neat stacks of cut grain, easily gathered for binding into sheaves. However, the gracefully beautiful wooden American grain cradles require a bent posture for ideal performance and can force undue stress on back muscles. A European bow-type cradle, though it leaves cut grain a little less neat, is lighter and can be used from an erect position. The bow that catches the grain is made from a strip of flexible wood that can be removed from the scythe when you are mowing hay or cutting grass.

My preference for reaping the garden-size bread patch is a sickle, and my favorite sickle, the Japanese *kama*, is especially suited for grain planted in rows rather than broadcast. The kama has a straight handle, about sixteen inches long. At a right angle to this is a straight, high-quality, forged carbon-steel blade about six inches long. Where most American and European sickles have long, curved blades, with points that point right at you, there is no danger of poking yourself with a kama. My other favorite sickle is an Austrian blade, with a finely serrated, razor-sharp edge.

When harvesting grain with a sickle, it is not necessary to swing a big arc, or to hack at the straw. With a sharp blade, you need only grasp a handful of grain stalks in your left hand and cut the straw by deftly pulling the sharp (yes, keep it sharp) blade through the bundles that you hold. Then lay the handful an arm's length behind you to the left, out of the way where you won't step through it as you move down the row. Make neat piles as you go to facilitate binding into sheaves later. If there are a lot of green weeds growing in your grain crop, avoid as many as you can as you reap; tied into the sheaves they will slow the curing and drying of the grain and increase the likelihood of fungus growth.

If you have planted a larger plot and broadcast your seed, try to find a good European scythe with a bow-type grain cradle. You'll work standing instead of squatting, the work will take one-third the time that the sickle takes, and the cut grain will be left in straight windrows, with all the cut ends lined up, ready for binding into sheaves.

SHEAVES AND SHOCKS

However you choose to reap your crop, the next step is to bind it into sheaves and stack these sheaves into shocks, or stooks as they are called in some parts, for further ripening and curing before threshing. Twine works well for binding, but a more natural choice is right at hand: the straw itself. A dozen or so straws, wrapped around your fist to make them more flexible, will, when wrapped around a sheaf of grain and tied in an overhand knot, hold the sheaf as well as any twine, though it does take some practice to get it right.

How big is a sheaf? Well, that depends some on how long your straw is, I reckon. I had trouble making tight sheaves until I read David Tresemer's *The Scythe Book* (Hand and Foot, 1981). Instead of using brittle straw he suggests a green weed or two from the field's edge. Tresemer describes his technique thus: "Encircle the sheaf with the binder of straw or weed until the top and bottom of the binder overlap. Holding onto the very bottom of the binder, slip its top

11

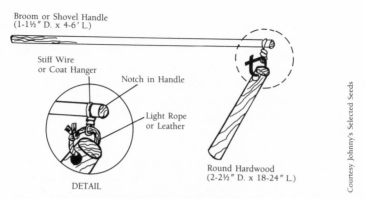

Broom or Shovel Handle
(1-1½" D. x 4-6' L.)

Stiff Wire
or Coat Hanger

Notch in Handle

Light Rope
or Leather

Round Hardwood
(2-2½" D. x 18-24" L.)

DETAIL

Courtesy Johnny's Selected Seeds

CONSTRUCTION OF A FLAIL

under its own base in a half hitch. Slide this half hitch along the base until the sheaf is bound tight. Bend the stiffer base of the binder back over the half hitch and tuck it under itself against the sheaf." Tresemer also suggests an aid for use in tightening and holding the sheaves while binding. "A *woolder.* . .is a block of wood two inches square with a 36-inch piece of twine through a hole in the middle. One end of the twine is knotted so it is tight against the wood; the other end is wound around the sheaf and then around the twine beneath the wood block."

To make a shock or stook, lean six to ten sheaves against each other in a circle. To keep the sheaves from falling over, as John Seymour in *The Guide to Self-Sufficiency* (Hearst Books, 1976) suggests, rub the heads of two neighboring sheaves together so the heads intermesh. To protect from rain, cap each stock with an extra-large sheaf. If persistent or heavy rain threatens, cover the shocks with waterproof material or move them under cover.

THRESHING AND WINNOWING

Once the straw has turned completely yellow and the grain is hard and dry, your crop is ready for threshing, though if it is under cover and safe from rodent snacking, you can do this at your leisure. Threshing will shake or knock the grain itself from the heads, but will not, unless you are using a threshing machine with screens, separate the wheat from the chaff. A small amount of grain can be easily threshed by the "barrel method." Untie the sheaves, grasp a handful of straw at the base, and beat the heads against the inside of a clean and dry drum or barrel. After a dozen or two strokes check the head; if no kernels remain, grasp another handful and repeat until your job is finished. The barrel method has an advantage over the traditional flailing method that follows in that the straw does not become mixed with the grain.

For thousands of years the flail has been the primary threshing tool. When one considers the 10,000 odd years since the advent of granoculture, and the rather late introduction of mechanized threshers, it may well be that more grain has been threshed with a flail than with threshers and combines together. Many early American barns had a "threshing floor": a large wooden deck, with boards carefully fitted so that there were no cracks for grains of wheat, oats, or barley to fall through. Here, the loosened sheaves were spread, and the threshers would "flail" them until the grain was loosened from the heads.

Although several types of flails have been used for this purpose, the most common design, and one in use at least since the early days of the Christian era, is simply two poles of wood, as thick as a shovel handle, one six feet long and the other eighteen inches, loosely attached, end-to-end, with a leather thong. The best leather is of eelskin—tough, pliable, and long-lasting. While such tools are, alas, no longer available at the village market, you can make a reasonable facsimile yourself with materials likely already at hand. The short piece of wood, the swingle, should be of hardwood. A tangle-proof method of joining as suggested by Rob Johnston, Jr., president of Johnny's Selected Seeds, is illustrated on page 12. The wire should turn freely in the groove on the handle. Sturdy, reinforced twine will substitute for eelskin, but check frequently for wear: a hardwood swingle can be a dangerous projectile.

If you lack a threshing floor, spread a large tarpaulin or heavy sheet on level ground and spread the unbound sheaves in the middle. If you're threshing only a small amount of grain, the straw can be wrapped loosely in a tarp or enclosed in a large fabric bag to keep the grains from scattering. The idea is less to beat the grains from the heads than it is to shake them loose from a thick (twelve-inch) pile of straw. Raise the handle of the flail until the swingle is shoulder high, then bring it down firmly so that the swingle strikes with its full length against the straw. The arms should be slightly bent at the elbows and relaxed, the back straight. The motion should be from the shoulders, repeated rhythmically. Two or more threshers working together beat a strong cadence, the rhythm for many a threshing chant. Rather than striking from a stationary position, shift your feet in a simple dance, first one foot forward as you strike, then the other. When no grain remains in the heads, lift off the long straw and reserve for mulch, compost, weaving, or thatching.

The remaining grain, chaff, and small bits of straw are ready for winnowing. The simplest method of cleaning is all that is needed for small lots of grain harvested from weed-free patches. In a steady wind, pour the grain from one container to another, varying the distance between them according to weight of grain and strength of wind. Lacking wind and the patience to wait, an electric fan is a satisfactory substitute. In *Farmers of Forty Centuries*, King described a manually operated Japanese winnowing fan. Becalmed farmers of early America used a winnowing sheet, though it took forty-five minutes to clean only a bushel of wheat this way. For over 2,000 years the Chinese have used a winnowing machine, or fanning mill. Virtually all of today's commercial grain is cleaned with a machine little changed from the venerable one of Cathay.

In a fanning mill the grain first passes over the top or "scalping" screen, which is of a mesh that permits passage of the grain and anything its size or smaller. Large bits of straw, weeds, and large weed seeds are "scalped" off the top. The grain falls into the grading screen below, which has a mesh too small for the plump grain to fall through, but undersize kernels, small weed seeds, dust and bits of chaff and straw are separated from the grain. Finally the grain passes through a blast of air that blows away the remaining light dirt, chaff, and straw. Small hand- or motor-powered fanning mills are still manufactured today, and used ones are frequently found at farm auctions. Screens of various mesh size are available for cleaning different grains. If you want to scalp and grade your wind-winnowed grain, the task is easily performed with a series of sieves or riddles screened with the proper mesh.

Though few farmers, even self-providers, carry out the final step that follows, nineteenth-century whole foods advocate Sylvester Graham considered it essential in making good bread and affirmed that once having baked with washed wheat, the home baker would use nothing else. You may find the better flavor worth the extra effort. In a bucket, cover the grain with clean cold water, stir briskly and drain immediately. Spread to dry in sheets in the sun or on racks or screens in a warm and breezy spot.

The simple tools and processes described above are sufficient for home-grown wheat, rye, hull-less oats, and hull-less barley. Hulled barley and oats, millet, rice, and buckwheat require further milling beyond the scope of this chapter. Buckwheat flour can be easily made from unhulled buckwheat by grinding the grain and sifting to remove the large flakes of hull, resulting in a dark-flecked flour.

STORING YOUR GRAIN

Be sure your grain is dry before storing. If you are unsure, even though it seems hard and crunchy, spread to dry for a day or two before storage. Grain with a moisture content below 13.5 percent can be stored indefinitely without risk of spoilage. Seasoned farmers and millers can judge the amount of moisture to within a tenth of a percentage point from a single bite. If you want to be certain, take a bucketful to your local grain elevator. They have a tester and the charge will be nominal.

Small amounts of grain can be stored in jars and cans, larger quantities in bags or barrels. While it is ideal that grain be stored under cool and dry conditions, it is *essential* that it be stored dry—not in a damp corner of the basement. Freezing weather will do no harm, and will, in fact, kill insects, but do be sure that your storage is rodent-proof. Even if mice and rats take only a little bit from your granary, they will likely urinate on some of what they leave.

Studies performed at the Benson Institute of Brigham Young University have shown that dry ice can reduce insect infestation of small grains in home storage. Place a piece of the solid carbon dioxide in the bottom of your airtight storage container, fill with clean, dry grain, leave covered loosely until the dry ice is nearly vaporized, then seal. The low-oxygen environment that results will not support insect respiration. If insects do hatch out in your stored grain, they can be killed by freezing the grain, and removed by regrading and winnowing.

Some European traditions give the first loaf of a new crop back to the field. Given your small patch, I think the Goddess will find a small wheaten roll acceptable.

RESOURCES

Good Seed Co.
Star Rt., Box 73A
Oroville, WA 98844
(catalog $1.00; stocks open-pollinated seeds, heirloom varieties, and general garden supplies)

I-Tech
P.O. Box 795
Davis, CA 95617
(SASE with request for information on seed thresher and other hand-operated tools)

Woodline: The Japan Woodworker
1731 Clement Ave.
Alameda, CA 94501
(catalog $1.00; carries the Japanese kama and woodworking tools)

Smith & Hawken
25 Corte Madera
Mill Valley, CA 94941
(catalog free; carries hand-made gardening tools and accessories)

Plow and Hearth
Rt. 10, Box 112
Charlottesville, VA 22901
(catalog free; scythes and gardening tools)

A. M. Leonard
P.O. Box 816
Piqua, OH 45356
(catalog free; has scythes and sickles and supplies for professional horticulturists)

In-Tec Equipment
Box 123
D. V. Station
Dayton, OH 45406
(send SASE for information on homesteading and small-farm equipment)

THE RETURN OF
OLD GRAIN MILLS

T
HE SLOW RUMBLE OF TURNING WHEELS OF
WOOD, STEEL, AND STONE, THE SOFT CREAK
OF WELL-GREASED WOODEN COGS, AND THE
gentle splash of water have been the music of John Murphy's life for
half a century. But soon the mill song will stop and the wheels turn
no more, marking the end of a master miller's life work and the close
of an era for the tiny village of Foulksmill, County Wexford, in
southeast Ireland. The farm families who have brought their home-
grown grain here to be ground since Richard Purcell built the mill in
1851 will soon buy their feed from the farmers' cooperative and their
bread flour from the grocer. They will thus follow the pattern of most
of Ireland, where the advent of the steam engine and later electricity
ended the reign of the waterwheel as the main power for grinding the
grain for daily bread.

Now only eight commercial flour mills remain in all of the Irish
Republic and even fewer small custom mills still grind for the local
populace. In 1982 nearly 20 percent of Ireland's 240,000 tons of flour
were imported from the United Kingdom. In addition to this 45,000
tons of imported flour, Irish millers imported 120,000 tons of wheat
from North America, the United Kingdom, and France. Two-thirds of
the wheat for Irish bread was grown abroad.

The decline of the local water-powered mill is not limited to Ireland, but is just as evident throughout Europe and North America. In
the United States there were over 16,000 mills at work in 1886, as
reported in *Cawkers Biennial Flour Mill Directory* of that year. In 1983

the Society for the Preservation of Old Mills in Knoxville, Tennessee, listed 169 "stone-ground" watermills in operable condition in the United States. Only a handful actually operate as full-time milling businesses. The remainder are maintained or have been restored by individuals or organizations as "monuments to the age of water."

As awareness grows about the importance of developing local and regional food systems and the inherent economic and ecologic benefits of free, non-polluting flowing water as a power source, will the watermill once again emerge as an essential element in many rural communities? Will the growing recognition of the value of whole grains help to halt the decline of small mills? Is the watermill destined to extinction or to rebirth as part of a network joining agriculture and food processing in a sustainable future?

Michael LaForest, editor and publisher of *Old Mill News*, the quarterly journal of the Society for the Preservation of Old Mills, says "The Society is not in a position to give direct aid to someone wanting to refit an old mill, but through the Society people can get technical advice, and we may be able to help them locate old equipment they need. Just that we exist gives people an affinity with others interested in old mills. It can really help to know that you're not alone." Has the society helped to slow the demise of the watermill? LaForest thinks so. He says, "There are mills working now that weren't ten or fifteen years ago."

WATER AND STONE

For two thousand years millers have harnessed moving water to turn the heavy stones used for grinding grain. But people crushed grains for bread and porridge for uncounted thousands of years before the development of the waterwheel and its subsequent use to power revolving millstones. The earliest grain mill was probably a hand-held stone, with which the "miller" would strike the grain, using a broad, flat stone as an anvil. If the same bottom stone were used continuously, the pounding would very slowly form a hollow in its center. As this became deeper it would be necessary to replace the rounded hand stone with a longer "pestle." Eventually, mortars came to be cut and shaped for their specific purpose.

The other long-surviving mill to emerge from that original primitive system is the saddlestone, a broad, slightly concave stone used in conjunction with an oblong hand-held stone. Grain was reduced by pushing and pulling the handstone over the grains, which rested in the shallow concave. The saddlestone was the first *grinding* mill; the earlier pounder and primitive mortar and pestles were tools for *crushing* grain, yielding coarse meal at best. Developed during paleolithic times, the saddlestone remained the best—and most widely used—tool for grinding cereals through the Neolithic era and was the premier mill of classical Greek civilization. In Rome this became the *mola trusatilis*, the thrusting mill.

The next significant step in milling came with the development of the rotary "quern," made of two round, flat stones and a turning handle. The quern was basically a small household mill, but the rotary grinding principle was applied to mills turned by slaves or by animals. Thus was born *mola asinarias*, a mill powered by an ass. The next step in the evolution of grain milling was the application of water power to turn the rotary millstones. The various forms of rotary mills, querns, ass mills, and slave mills were all in use at the time of Christ. And though waterwheels were in use in some remote parts of the empire and beyond its borders for at least a hundred years before that, they did not become the principal mills of Rome for another century or two. The relatively large capital investment required for building a water mill and the plentiful supply of slave labor combined to slow the spread of water power through the Roman Empire.

The actual origin of the waterwheel is uncertain. According to Joseph Needham, author of the multi-volume *Science and Civilization in China* (Cambridge University Press), it is equally ancient in Asia Minor and in China. By the time of Christ it was known in classical southern Europe. The earliest known watermill was working in 65 B.C. when the last Mithridates of Pontus (Persia) was overthrown by Pompeii. It became part of history when included in a list of the ruler's forfeited property which was compiled by Strabo forty years later.

At about the same time that the waterwheel reached Japan from China, water-driven grain mills appeared in Ireland, the westernmost land in Europe. By this time they had spread along the coast of Europe, northward to Scandinavia. By the end of the first millennium after Christ, watermills could be found on almost every running stream in all hilly parts of Europe and adjoining lands. The *Domesday Book* (1080-1086) recorded over 5,000 mills operating in England nine hundred years ago.

In 1781 John Smeaton, an English engineer, wrote that the steam engine was too "rough-running and liable to stoppages" to be used reliably for the milling of grain, that the engines "lacked the regularity and continuous rate of speed necessary for grinding corn." These recalcitrant and unreliable motors were, however, used indirectly to power mills by driving pumps to lift water from below the mill dam back up into the mill pond, thus assuring a full head of water and a constant and steady supply. Three years later, the steam engine had been improved enough to encourage the building of the world's first steam-driven flour mill. James Watt's Albion Mill in London began operation in 1784, boasting thirty-six pairs of stones powered by two fifty-horsepower steam engines. Although the Albion Mill was destroyed by fire only seven years later, it was the first mill of a new era, and marked the beginning of the end of the 2,000-year reign of the water-powered mill for grinding grain.

The "stone age" of milling lasted for thousands of years, but in the late eighteenth and early nineteenth centuries experimental work with the use of steel rollers for grinding flour was being carried out. In the mid-1830s the first successful roller mill began milling in Switzerland. In 1862 a mill in Ipswich, England, was built that used steel rollers in combination with stone grinding. In 1870 Vernons Mill at Birken Head, Liverpool, became the first all-roller mill in Britain. The first roller mills in the United States were built nine years later in Minneapolis. Some of these early roller mills used porcelain rollers for the final crushing of the meal into flour, but hardened steel rollers soon replaced these. A century later only a small fraction of our flour is ground on stone; the stone age has at last ceded to the age of steel.

The slave mill and ass mill removed milling from the home. Water-powered mills removed milling from the bakery, and the steam engine allowed the removal of milling from the local streamside to the international dockside. But technology alone does not determine the direction of economic development. The adaptation of motor power to milling could have meant, and did in some isolated cases, that grinding grain need not be restricted to locations with flowing water and may have brought greater decentralization. But instead, the application of steam power to milling moved the flour mill from the village to the great ports, as flour became more an element of national and international trade.

It is important to note that this is not a strict sequential history. Saddlestones remain in use today in certain parts of the Americas, coincident with the latest high-speed, multiple-break roller mill in Kansas City. The quern continued to be used throughout the development of various types of watermills and, like the saddlestone, is still in use today. The most primitive forms of horizontal waterwheels were being built in mountainous regions of the southern United States as highly effective turbines were being built in Europe. And all of these earlier forms of mills were in use when the steam-powered Albion Mill went on line in 1784.

Though built in 1851, more than a half century after the American inventor Oliver Evans first introduced to mills such labor-saving devices as the elevator and the conveyor, Richard Purcell's new five-story mill in Foulksmill had none of these improvements. One hundred and thirty-five years later it still doesn't. John Murphy operates the mill alone using the same simple machinery that has been in use since the 1850s—a teacle (miller's windlass or winch) for hoisting the bags of grain and meal from loft to loft, a simple grain cleaner, and two millstones, one each for barley and wheat. And though this mill was built half a century after the steam-powered Albion Mill across the Celtic Sea, it is powered entirely by the falling water of an adjacent stream. Originally there were two more stones, a second for wheat and one for shelling oats, but these were removed a few years before Murphy moved to Foulksmill. As country people began to rely more on bakeries for their bread and to prefer quick-cooking "oatlets" to stone-ground oatmeal for their morning porridge, the grinding of barley for animal feed gained prominence in the daily work at the mill.

A MILLER AT WORK

But even with these changes, John Murphy's day is little different from the day of the millers that preceded him here. After wheeling his heavy black bicycle through the red wooden door, he climbs two flights of open stairs to the third "loft" (mill talk for floor), empties a bag of cleaned wheat onto the floor above the wheat mill on the "stone loft" one floor below, descends to the stone loft and checks the flow of wheat into the mill hopper as he passes the four-foot-diameter, wood-housed millstones on his way to the back door. Outside, he cranks open the wooden gate above the millrace, and the five-foot-wide, twelve-foot-high breastwheel (so-called because the water strikes it at breast level), slowly begins to turn as its buckets fill with the clear, chilly water. The wheel reaches its ideal speed, and Murphy makes a final adjustment in the gate opening and returns to the half-light of the mill.

As the sun rises above the hill behind the village, dust-laden shafts of light fall across the well-worn floor. Until he breaks for his midday meal, Murphy's time is consumed with the working of the mill: lift grain, run it through the cleaner into a bag, lift the bag to the floor above, with a handtruck move the bag to a four-inch square hole in the floor, push the bag over, spilling contents into a pile on the floor around the hole. The grain flows down the hole, through a chute and "sock" made from a burlap bag into the hopper of the stone mill. As the mill grinds, the level in the hopper remains constant—as long as the grain is kept piled above the hole, a condition that requires frequent attention. The flour runs directly into a bag on the ground floor below the millstones, or, if the customer requests, first through a sifting device (powered by the waterwheel) that removes the largest flakes of bran.

It sounds pretty simple, with little work involved: just dump a bag of wheat into the hopper of the cleaner—it collects in another bag on the floor below. Use the water-powered teacle to hoist the bag up to the floor above, roll it over to the hole above the mill, dump, and let gravity take over from there. Here's the hitch: the mill can grind about 400 pounds of wheat into fine flour in an hour. If each bag holds about 100 pounds, that's one bag to dump every fifteen minutes. And the cleaner runs at the same time. So that's four more bags to dump each hour. And the flour bag on the ground floor fills—and has to be replaced—four times an hour. Don't forget that the grain has to be kept pushed over the hole in the floor or the mill hopper will run empty, causing the stones to grind against each other and possibly ruin the grinding surfaces. (Such damage could take the better part of a day to repair and can take years off the life of the stones.) Finally, bags of cleaned grain have to be hoisted back up to the floor above.

This all happens on three different floors. John Murphy moves from one floor to another, always keeping everything running smoothly. And he does it with unhurried ease, performing each task with instinctual perfection, treading lightly on well-worn wooden stairs comfortably shaped by his own feet after forty years.

Ann Redmond, a silver-haired great-granddaughter of Richard Purcell, now lives in the mill house a hundred yards behind the mill. In 1985, over a meal of boiled cabbage, potatoes, and her own "brown cake" (whole-meal soda bread), she related, with not-quite-concealed sorrow, that her children are all grown and none really took an interest in the mill. "We thought of trying to keep it going," she said, "maybe grind flour to sell, but there's permits that we've not needed, since we only grind what people bring us. We don't sell anything, only charge for the milling. And the mill has been losing money. We're sorry to close it. Sorry for the mill and sorry for John." The Redmonds have chosen this year to close the mill because now Murphy will be eligible for his old-age pension.

John Murphy's life of milling in County Wexford is drawing to a close because he is retiring. The mill still provides an important service for the small farmers around Foulksmill, grinding their barley and wheat for feed and flour. The waterwheel at Richard Purcell's mill is stopping after 135 years due to circumstances that range far beyond the farms around Foulksmill, County Wexford, or even Ireland. Each year, fewer farmers bring their barley here to be milled for feed. Most sell their grain at harvest and buy rations from the dairy cooperative. Few households still bake their own bread, and most that do prefer the convenience of store-bought two-kilo bags. The village mill, an essential link in the subsistence society, serves little purpose in the buy and sell atmosphere of today's consumer economy. The Redmond family has been losing money for the past few years—not much, granted, but the family farm has been subsidizing John's salary, and with the current slump in farm prices that's a service that the Redmonds can ill afford.

DOES STONE-GROUND MAKE A DIFFERENCE?

"He told me how in the big mill where he works the grindin'
is all done by steam, and the machines runs so fast an' gits so hot,
an' burns all the taste out-a the flour. 'They is no real bread but
what's made out-a water-ground flour,' he says to me."

—Till Blake in Sapphira
and the Slave Girl
by Willa Cather

Many bakers and natural foods advocates insist on stone-ground flour, pointing to its texture, sweet-nutty flavor, supposedly higher nutritional value, and better overall baking qualities compared to steel roller-milled flour. They credit the "natural" grinding surface, the gentle grinding operation, and the lower heat generated during milling as major contributors to stone-ground flour's superiority.

No doubt many of these bakers have had superb results using stone-ground flour, but are the reasons for their claims accurate? And what about a third method in which the grain is pulverized by rapidly spinning metal hammers? Let's look at these three methods of making flour and how the different machines may affect the finished product.

In a hammer mill grain flows into a chamber where it is pulverized by rapidly spinning steel hammer blades until the particles are of uniform size. They then pass through the holes in the screen that surrounds the milling chamber. Because there is a high ratio of air to wheat in the chamber, excessive heat is not a problem, although oxidation may be. The most recently developed of these three methods of milling, hammer milling is used primarily for grinding feed and by natural foods companies. The latter use it to produce fine whole-grain flour with no large flakes of bran, a texture preferred by some bakers for pastries and deemed necessary for some pasta shaped by forcing dough through specially shaped dies.

A roller mill is basically a set of steel wringers through which grain passes and is crushed. Most of the flour for supermarkets and bakeries is produced on mills of this type. In a modern flour mill, the grain passes through a series of rollers and separators. The grain is gradually reduced from whole grains to fine flour. As the milling proceeds, the germ and bran are removed from the endosperm, the starchy, gluten-rich center of the berry. Although the roller mills were designed and are primarily used for producing highly refined white flour, some mills make whole wheat flour by regrinding the coarse "shorts"—bran and germ—and mixing them back in with the flour.

A stone mill consists of two circular stones—one a stationary "bedstone" and one a revolving "runner stone." Whole grain enters at the center and is cut and ground by the shearing action of the grooves in the stones. The grain gradually moves outward due to centrifugal force. By the time the grain reaches the edge of the stone it has become flour.

The most common charge against roller milling is that excessive heat is generated, thereby destroying some of the nutrients and adversely affecting both the flavor and the baking qualities of the flour. Is this judgment justified?

ADM Flour Milling operates twenty big "gradual reduction, multiple break" flour mills across the United States. At their mill in Inman, Kansas, they produce both conventional roller-milled white flour and stone-ground whole wheat flour, the latter ground on a mill with a pair of thirty-inch stones. In January of 1985, at my request, ADM ran temperature checks on two different days for both types of flour. The whole wheat flour was, in both cases, twenty degrees warmer than the roller-milled white flour. However, the high temperature of the two stone-ground samples was 116°F, still below the 120°F point at which nutrient levels may begin to be affected. Even in the heat of summer the hottest flour from the roller mills, according to John Landis, vice president in charge of operations, won't exceed 100°F, and the rolls themselves stay between 100°F and 110°F. Landis says that in a stone mill the grain is reduced from whole grain to flour in one pass. The friction between grain and stone generates heat, which is stored in the massive granite stones. Roller milling is a gradual reduction process. That is, the wheat is reduced in steps from whole to flour. The heat build-up is avoided because the milling friction is spread over a number of rolls, each successive set of rollers crushing the wheat into finer particles.

There are stone mills that generate less heat than the ADM roller mills, generally slower turning "flat runners" (horizontal stones) rather than the more commonly used and faster "edge runners" (vertical stones). And any well-dressed (sharpened) stone will grind cooler than if dull. Thus, the difference appears not to be one of heat, although it is hard to ignore statements from bakers based on their experience.

Jean Ponce, head baker at Ponce French Bakery in Chico, California, grinds his own flour in a stone mill at the bakery. He's not concerned about the heat, he says, though "sometimes the mill may grind a little hot because I let the grain feed through a little too fast or because I have the stones set a little too close. No, heat is not a problem. But roller mills? In a stone mill wheat is cut and rolled and ground between two stones. In a roller mill, the grain is squeezed and squeezed again. This is not milling, this is not flour. I cannot make real bread without flour."

Hy Lerner, owner of Baldwin Hill Bakery in Phillipston, Massachusetts, emphasizes the importance of using stone-ground flour for making his European style sourdough bread. For the first several years the bakery obtained flour—stone-ground from organic wheat— from a natural foods distributor. One batch of flour resulted in bread "like pancakes," a far cry from Baldwin Hill's usually light loaves. After eliminating all other variables, the problem was traced to the flour. But what was different about it? Lerner called his supplier and eventually discovered that their stone mill was out of service and they had contracted with another company for their flour milling. As it turned out, that company used a hammer mill to grind the whole wheat flour that had made the flat breads. Lerner found another source of stone-ground flour and the bread was back to normal. To avoid a repeat occurrence the bakery soon acquired its own mill and has since ground all its own flour.

Although there appear to be distinct differences among flours milled by different processes, these differences are largely undocumented. Steel rolls, steel hammers, and revolving stones may indeed impart their own signature to the flour they produce. These qualities are attested to from individual experience, invaluable in making decisions, but it would be helpful to be able to balance these with scientific research.

THE REBIRTH OF LOCAL MILLS

As John Murphy prepares to close the sluice gate of the Purcell mill for the final time, thirty miles away Oliver Mosse has opened the gate to the newly refitted Killenny Mill, at Kells in County Kilkenny. Idle for the last decade and a half, the newly dressed stones now grind fourteen tons of whole wheat flour each week, mostly for sale to bakeries in County Kilkenny. Mosse and his partner, Suzi Taylor, spent over a year cleaning the five-story stone building, building bulk storage bins and new stairways, installing new (used) elevators and conveyors. A new waterwheel was built and new bearings cast for the millstones themselves. After a long and sometimes frustrating year, the first "Kells Wholemeal" flowed from between the French burr-stones as the new waterwheel churned in the rushing water of the Kings River weir.

The Killenny Mill is but one of over a thousand that once ground grain in Ireland, and its revival does not necessarily mean that others will follow. But if Taylor and Mosse prove successful in their venture, others may be willing to try. A few mills in other parts of Ireland have been maintained in operable condition, while others are certainly re-storable. Twenty-four mills the size of Killenny could supply all the whole meal used in Ireland. Three hundred fifty could meet the entire flour needs. These same 350 mills would provide work for some one thousand people, roughly the same number now employed by the Irish flour-milling industry.

Ireland is not alone in losing her local mills to the advantage of centralized merchant milling, nor is she unique in now having the conditions that may lead to the rebirth of local mills. Most of Western Europe and North America is experiencing a strong and growing awareness of the value of whole-grain products for good health. There is a revival of local bakeries making traditional breads. A local mill is able to cater to the particular needs of these small, craft-oriented breadmakers, while the distant roller mills may offer only a few stand-ardized mixes. Just as changing social and economic conditions have nearly eliminated the local mill from our countryside and small towns, the new post-industrial era may provide the climate favorable for their return.

When I asked John Murphy about the future of small mills, he was hopeful. He said, "You'll be surprised. . .in a few years, maybe ten, they'll be starting up again around the country. There's a demand for whole meal now that we haven't seen for quite a while, and it's getting bigger. The big mills can't grind it the way these old stones know how." As he turns and gives the rope a gentle tug with his left hand, engaging the teacle, a hundred pound sack of cleaned local wheat emerges through the trap door in the floor. As this master miller wheels it over to the hole above the hopper, I wonder if the old waterwheel just needs a rest, and will soon turn again to grind the Wexford wheat.

RATING THE HOME GRAIN MILLS

THE FIRST LOAF OF BREAD I BAKED SOME TWENTY YEARS AGO WAS MADE FROM FRESHLY MILLED FLOUR. NO BREAD HAD EVER TASTED so nutty and rich, nor reminded me so much of the wheat fields of my childhood, as this loaf, still warm from the oven. Since then I've always tried to bake with the freshest flour, ground sometimes only minutes before mixing the dough. And since then I have searched for the perfect mill for home grinding. Numerous home grain mills have come onto the market in recent years, and I have tried to use most of them.

There are other advantages to milling your own flour than the superior flavor that only fresh-ground grain can give to your loaves. The oil in grains can quickly go rancid once grain is ground into flour. Grains are rich in B vitamins, but these are diminished by oxidation when whole grains are milled to make flour. Most stores sell only a limited range of flour, from wheat, rye, and corn. With your own mill you can grind whole-grain flour, meal, and cereals from millet, buckwheat, barley, oats, and amaranth as well. You grow your own grain, but the village mill down by the river closed up shop a century ago? With your own mill, you can have bread from your own patch, like great-great grandmother did.

The choice of mills is wide. They range from thirty-dollar hand-operated mills with steel grinding plates to $800 electric mills with native granite stones that can grind a hundred pounds of bread flour in an hour. Between these two extremes are high-tech plastic boxes with surgical steel "micronizing" grinding units and traditionally designed, slow-turning stone mills with beautifully finished wooden housings.

While most mills with steel plates can grind wet products and oily nuts and seeds as well as grain, stone mills are limited to the milling of dry grains.

Most home grain mills, whether hand- or motor-powered, whether equipped with stones or steel plates, operate in the same basic manner. The grain is poured into a hopper and feeds between the grinding surfaces. One plate or stone is stationary, the other rotates. The sharp cutting edges cut or crush the grain, breaking it into small pieces. The space between the two surfaces diminishes toward their perimeter. By the time the grain reaches the edge of the grinding surface it is reduced to flour. The fineness of grind is controlled by adjusting the space between the two plates or stones. All of the mills I tested except the Kitchen Mill and the Magic Mill (described later) operate in this manner.

But how do you choose a home mill? There are many on the market, but few in stores. Most are available only through mail order, and many advertise only in obscure publications or not at all. Can manufacturers' claims be believed?

To answer these questions, I requested models from various manufacturers and distributors of both electric and manual mills. I then set up a performance test, to which all the mills were submitted. To test the mills I ground 2½ pounds (the flour from this would be sufficient for a small batch of naturally leavened bread) of hard spring wheat in each. I recorded how long each mill took to grind the sample and measured the temperature of the wheat before grinding and the last flour to come out of the mill. I also ground samples of soft wheat, flint corn, and dent corn in each of the mills.

The flour from each of the mills was used to make a small batch of naturally leavened (Flemish-style *desem*) bread. The flour from all mills performed satisfactorily and all breads were delicious.

All but a few of the models reviewed here were generously loaned by either the manufacturers or distributors.

The observations that follow are often subjective, but I have also included objective criteria important to anyone choosing a home grain mill. First, I tried to judge the quality of wheat flour that a home grain mill is capable of producing. In addition to being able to produce good flour from both hard and soft wheat, a mill should also be able to grind corn into relatively fine meal. Another consideration is whether calories or kilowatts is the power source. Also, can the same mill grind both dry grain and wet material? Is it easy to clean, pleasant to look at, and quiet enough so that it doesn't drive you out of the room? How affordable is it? These and other criteria are important to consider before purchasing a hand or electric grain mill.

ELECTRIC MILLS

Kootenay Natural Stone Mills Model A-200

When *East West* publisher Leonard Jacobs returned from a trip to the West Coast with a brochure describing a collection of beautiful mills made by a company in British Columbia, I must confess it was love at first sight. Unfortunately, subsequent experiences with this model of Kootenay turned out to be something of a letdown.

These machines feature all-wood construction, "flat-running" (horizontal) stones, with "Sexton Mill Stones" quarried in South Tyrol. The mills appear to be scaled-down replicas of the ones I had seen operating in centuries-old water-powered mills in Europe. The brochure claimed that the slow-turning stones produced cool flour, even after hours of grinding. The prices were high, but all who had seen them and the one person I talked to who had used a Kootenay Natural Stone Mill were enthusiastic. Most models of Kootenay mills are designed for various scales of commercial use, but the smallest in their standard line, the A-200, with an hourly output of 11-13 pounds of fine flour, looked to be the cream of the small mills and ideal for family use.

Perhaps any time you have expectations as high as what I had built up for this—and I waited weeks for delivery by truck from the West Coast—you can expect disappointment. The wooden body of the mill, though structurally sound, is not of the quality of wood that I

Left: The Samap F-100 is powerful, convenient, and easy to clean. Above: Hawo's mills are finely crafted and grind small grains with ease.

had expected in a mill that costs as much as this: softwood with quite a few knots, though none seemed to present more than cosmetic problems, and some people like knotty pine. A few of the moving wooden parts are of hard maple. The sleeve that guides the grain from the hopper into the cavity in the center of the stones is of turned, wide-grain softwood, and was broken upon arrival, split lengthwise along the grain in two pieces. Kootenay cheerfully replaced the piece, but using tight-grained maple for this thin, fragile piece would be an improvement.

As to the actual grinding performance, unlike *all* the other electric-powered mills that I tested, the Kootenay A-200 is cool grinding. The wheat going into the mill was 73°F, the flour coming out only 8° warmer, even with continuous grinding. Large (for a home mill) eight-inch diameter stones turning at only 180 revolutions per minute (rpm) permit a reasonable output with cool flour. For medium flour I found the output rate to be nearly twice what the literature claimed for fine flour.

But the mill does present some problems for home use. One of these is counter space. The A-200 needs 20½ inches by 16½ inches with at least three feet clear above the countertop, and at 65 pounds total weight, it's not something you'd want to move out from under the counter every time you want to mill a few pounds of flour. Another problem is the actual quality of the flour produced. Even at its finest setting and with a slow rate of feed, the mill produced only medium bread flour from hard spring wheat. Although I find this flour perfect for country-style, naturally leavened loaves, many home bakers might prefer the option of a finer grind.

When I spoke with George Baumann of Kootenay, in Kaslo, British Columbia, he had two comments on the coarse flour. First, he noted that the stones were cut in Europe, where coarser flour is used for whole-grain breads. Second, he said that with use, the stones would "wear in" and soon be producing a finer flour. Baumann also suggested that the coarse flour could be sifted and the coarser parts run through the mill again. I tried this with excellent results, but it took considerable time. Kootenay offers a sifting attachment for their larger mills, but it costs more than the A-200, making it impractical for the home miller.

Because the mill is scaled down from a larger model, it seems to require some of the same attention that a miller is able to give, but that a home baker might find frustrating. Adjusting for fineness of grind requires finding the proper balance between rate of feed of grain into the stones and the actual distance between the stones.

There were a couple of minor adjustments required to make the mill conveniently operable, but nothing that anyone with a modest degree of mechanical ability shouldn't be able to handle. The various modifications are all things that I would be more than willing to do were I grinding regularly for small-scale commercial use, but for occasional, even weekly, home use, I think most people expect a ready-to-use mill, especially for this kind of money.

The A-200, and the larger models in the Kootenay line, appear to be excellent, though expensive mills, for the serious miller. But for the home baker/miller with limited funds, there may be better choices.

Kootenay Natural Stone Mills "Mini Mill" Model A-130

Like its big sister, the Mini Mill is aesthetically pleasing with its natural quarried stones and housing made completely of wood. Only 10½ x 13 x 18 inches high, and light enough (24 pounds) to be moved out from under the kitchen cupboard when you're ready to grind, the Mini Mill would fit into almost anybody's kitchen space. The wood on my sample was of better quality than that of the A-200, and the curves of the turned wooden stone housing and the cut-outs in the mill base give this mill a softness lacking in the boxier larger mill. The five-inch diameter stone is driven directly by a .4 horsepower motor and turns at 1,680 rpm, over nine times as fast as its belt-driven counterpart. The mill produced finer flour than the A-200, and at a faster rate. Corn flour, as well as corn meal, can be produced from dent or flour corn. Hard flint corn makes a satisfactory meal, but not flour. Soft wheat was reduced to fluffy and light pastry flour with only flecks of bran. The flour at the end of grinding our sample had risen only 15°.

Adjustment for grind is simply made by rotating the hopper assembly and top stone and locking it in place with a maple peg inserted into a hole. Rate of feed is constant, the grain flowing through a half-inch hole in the bottom of the hopper and into the hole in the center of the stones. A large toggle switch makes it easy to switch the mill on and off, but for mill and user safety the "on" and "off" positions should be marked. Also, like the A-200 it has no built-in circuit breaker.

Overall, the mill is easy to use, compact, and will grind corn and all small grains into flour or meal of satisfactory quality. Where the A-200 falls short as a home mill, the Kootenay Mini Mill excels.

Samap Model F-50 and Model F-100

The French-made Samap mills, with their bright orange plastic motor housing, anodized aluminum mill body, and clear plastic columnar hoppers, lack the warm, natural appearance of the wooden Kootenay mills, but are sturdy, efficient, reliable, well-engineered mills. The F-50 and F-100 each take less than a square foot of counter space, are under twenty inches high, and weigh twenty and thirty pounds respectively. They are easy to clean, simple to operate (a complete instruction manual is included), and feature dust-free operation, with flour being discharged into either a twist-on glass jar or into a plastic bag. The see-through plastic hoppers allow you to know how much grain is left to be ground without having to cross the room to look into the hopper. The standard F-50 hopper holds barely 3½ cups, while the F-100 comes with an extension that doubles that capacity. Additional extensions can be added to increase the holding capacity of either mill.

The grinding stones of both electric Samap mills are of what I call "cast natural conglomerate." This differs from the synthetic stones found in most domestically produced mills and from the natural quarried and hewn stones used in the Kootenay and Meadows mills. Small pieces of naturally occurring basaltic rock from the Greek isle of Naxos are imbedded in a magnesite (natural magnesium carbonate) cement and cast, machined, and bonded to the high-grade aluminum casings. The resulting millstones are hard and durable, and will never (according to the distributor's literature) need to be sharpened under normal household use. The flour they produce is of a relatively uniform texture at the finest setting, or a somewhat flakier flour, ideal for bread making, with the top stone backed off slightly. The stones can be backed off further for producing coarser meal and grits.

The primary difference between the two Samap mills is that the F-50 has a half-horsepower motor while the F-100's is a full one-horse motor. When it comes to performance, this translates to an output rate nearly twice as fast for the more powerful F-100. The F-50 will not mill corn, only small grains like wheat, rye, barley, millet, and rice. While the F-100 is more than powerful enough to mill even the hardest corn, large kernels tend to get caught in the feed opening at the bottom of the hopper. No damage is caused to the mill, but it can be aggravating and can greatly increase the amount of time necessary to mill a pound of corn.

The small diameter (4-inch), high-speed stones are able to produce relatively cool flour due to a patented cooling and flour discharge turbine. The constant forcing of air through the milling chamber prevents the stones from building up excessive heat with continuous grinding. The use of air to move the flour keeps it light and fluffy and helps to keep it cool. While the milling chamber itself is self-cleaning, the plastic discharge chute and a special upper dust collection bag do need special attention after each grinding to remove residual flour that might attract vermin or mold.

The French manufacturers of the Samap mills have been making mills for over thirty years. In that time they seem to have worked the bugs out of their designs. I used an earlier version of the F-100 for three years with no trouble or complaints, save the sticking-corn-kernel problem. It ground hard and soft wheat equally well. The earlier model had more metal and less plastic, but otherwise the new mill seems identical. The mills come complete with grain scoops and flour bags, ready to plug in and go to work.

Jupiter Electric Cereal Grinder
(Stainless Steel and Stone Models)

The Jupiter Electric Cereal Grinders are small, inexpensive mills about the size of a small kitchen mixer. They use about the same amount of electricity as your overhead kitchen light. The power unit for these two mills is identical and is enclosed within a plastic housing. The motor is equipped with an overload cut-out.

While their rate of output is extremely slow, the quality of the finished flour, especially for the stainless steel model, is as good as more expensive, higher production models. The metal hopper for the stainless model holds only two pounds of wheat. Both hard and soft wheats were ground to powdery fine consistency, with small flakes of bran. The mill can be easily adjusted (even while running) to produce coarser flour, meal, or cracked grains for cereal. A common kitchen bowl fits easily beneath the discharge of the mill. Because the rate of output was relatively slow there was no problem with dust getting into the kitchen, but this would be a difficulty if there were a slight breeze. Even though the time required to grind the sample was a long eighteen minutes, the temperature of the last flour out of the mill was only 23° warmer than the wheat itself. At 103°F, it was certainly not approaching the temperature at which nutritional or enzymatic damage might occur.

Cleaning is easy: the grinding head disassembles quickly, and can be wiped or washed clean. The mill is light and compact. Broken down, it would fit in any deep kitchen drawer or on a shelf.

The stone version came equipped with stones of the same material as that of the Samap mills. While it produced flour of fine texture, it was quite slow and generated considerable heat. Like the stainless Jupiter, the stone version is easily adjustable, but doesn't produce coarser meals and grits of the same quality as the steel mill. Instead, it produces more of a mix of flour and larger particles of grain.

Neither of the Jupiter mills will grind corn.

Meadows Household Mill

For over eighty-five years the Meadows Mill Company has continued to manufacture stone burr mills in North Wilkesboro, North Carolina. They are at present the only company in the U.S. that makes a mill equipped with quarried natural stone burrs. Their natural granite stones are hewn from a nearby quarry and dressed at the mill factory.

While most of the Meadows line of grain mills is for commercial production (their largest will grind over 1,000 pounds of flour per hour), in 1950 they began to make a household mill with eight-inch stones. Some household mill: one hour's grinding will produce over one hundred pounds of whole wheat flour! Five pounds can be ground in less than four minutes, including set-up and adjustment of the mill. The mill with "assembly A" (wooden base with receiving drawer to hold six quarts of flour) takes up only slightly more room than the Kootenay A-200 and costs about the same. The mill is also available with a steel floor stand with provisions for catching the flour in a bag.

The mill looks like it was made by a small industrial company in North Carolina. The steel hopper and cast-iron mill body are painted with glossy white enamel, the wooden base and drawer front with standard industrial grey. It has its own sort of beauty, though I doubt it's one that many people would care to grace their kitchens with.

In grinding my 2½-pound sample, the temperature of the flour reached only 92°F, just a 16° rise from the wheat. However, with continuous grinding I measured temperatures as high as 118°F. That seems to be the limit with well-dressed stones and a reasonable rate of feed. If you should set the feed faster than the mill can handle, the motor is protected with an overload breaker.

The mill is easy to operate and comes with complete instructions, including guidelines for dressing the stones when they get dull. Adjustment of both rate of feed and fineness of grind are easily made by turning a large screw on the front of the mill. With the drawer completely closed, the operation of the mill is nearly dust-free.

Workhorse that the Meadows household mill may be, it does have its shortcomings. With heavy use the stones require frequent dressing. The Meadows factory will sharpen the stones for a nominal fee if you return the mill to them, but the shipping costs could be high, and you'd be without a mill for the time the mill was in transit.

If the mill is operated in a cool room, condensation problems can occur on the inside of the cast-iron housing. As the stones warm up from the friction of grinding, moisture is released from the flour as it is ground. This can condense on the inside of the cast housing. In turn, the flour sticks to the film of moisture, leaving a light patina of flour adhering to the inner wall of the mill. The mill comes apart fairly easily, but it's not a task you'd want to do on a weekly basis for a routine cleaning. If used regularly on a routine schedule, and in a moderately warm room, the condensation should not be a problem.

The eight-inch Meadows mill might be better classified as a community or small commercial mill than as a household tool. However, it is the only electric mill we tested that can grind, without difficulty or aggravation, all small grains, as well as hard and soft corn, into flours and meals of good quality.

Kitchenetics Kitchen Mill & Magic Mill III Plus

All the other electric flour mills I tested relied on some sort of stone to do the actual grinding of the grain, but not these two. The Magic Mill has "new micro-milling heads." The Kitchen Mill has a "micronetic milling chamber." In fact, both use different versions of the same basic grinding apparatus, a micronizer. First developed for use in the pharmaceutical industry, a micronizer consists of two surgical stainless steel discs with concentric rows of stainless steel teeth projecting inward. The two discs spin in opposite directions at the incredible speed of 28,000 rpm. The grain enters the micronizer at the center, is moved outwards by centrifugal force, and is propelled into the alternating rows of steel teeth spinning in opposite directions. The repeated impacts as the grain travels out from the center quickly reduce it to fine flour.

These two mills are near twins, both in mode of operation and in outward appearance. With their sleek modern looks and shiny plastic bodies, they'd look just perfect next to the food processor and hot-air popcorn popper on the textured Formica countertop. If the Kootenay looks like it belongs in a nineteenth-century watermill, and the Meadows in your father's 1950s workshop, these will look right at home in the future's high-tech kitchen.

The Magic Mill outperformed the Kitchen Mill on several counts. It is almost three times as fast, created less dust (the Kitchen Mill blew flour past its filter), was more willing to accept large kernels of corn, created less of a temperature rise, and held more grain in the hopper and more flour in the catch pan. Both produced extremely fine flour on their finest settings and flour surprisingly like finely milled stone-ground flour on the next-to-finest setting. Neither really produced, on any setting, anything that could pass for coarse meal or grits. These are flour mills.

The Lexan plastic mill body on the Kitchen Mill was cracked upon arrival, but it performed well regardless. While the Magic Mill has a stainless steel flour pan that locks in place with spring-loaded steel balls, the Kitchen has a smoke-tint Lexan pan that is held in place with molded clips on the side of the mill housing. I wouldn't trust these to continued use, especially considering the condition the mill arrived in. Plastic is not the most resilient and durable material under stress or tension.

I found these mills awkward to use—the milling unit may weigh only seven pounds but that's seven pounds that you don't have to move to get flour out of any of the other mills. When it came time to clean I couldn't figure out how to get the flour out from between all those tiny teeth, locked away beyond access.

Each of the manufacturers makes claims in their literature that my tests do not support. Kitchenetics literature claims "low temperature milling." "Since the mill has no rubbing surfaces to...cause friction, or get hot, the flour stays cooler than other mills," the brochure reads. In our tests, the Kitchen Mill's 37°F temperature rise ranks it third highest, behind the Magic Mill and Jupiter stone.

The makers of the Magic Mill claim their mill is "quieter...to use than other mills." I didn't have a sound level meter to measure the decibels emitting from either of these mills, but people came from three rooms away when I turned this one on. None of the electric mills were exactly what I would call quiet, but the high-pitched, jet-engine whine of the two micronizing mills was by far the most disturbing.

Like all the above mills, these two models have advantages and disadvantages that you'll have to consider. Both of these mills produced flour with good baking quality and good texture. They are fast, and on their finest setting make powder-like pastry flour that no other mill could match. But do you need such fine flour for anything but occasional pastry baking?

Hawo's Flour Mills

A recent entry in the U.S. market are two German-designed stone mills now being made by hawo's of Salmon Arm, British Columbia. These mills feature corundum stones imbedded in heat-hardened ceramic and finely crafted, oil-finished hardwood cabinets. In design and appearance, the models are nearly identical and have no major functional differences other than speed. The cabinet of the small hawo's is made of beech joined with tight-fitting box or finger joints at the corners. The larger model, which can be ordered in either beech or, for a small extra cost, oak, is joined with beautifully executed dovetail joints. Both models are finely crafted and attractively designed.

The small mill ground a hopper-full (1½ pounds) of hard spring wheat into fine bread flour in just under four minutes, while the larger model emptied its hopper of 2½ pounds of grain in just over five minutes. In grinding five pounds of flour, neither mill raised the temperature of the grain enough to cause any loss of its nutritional or baking qualities. The only major design feature that caused a problem was that the hopper holds more grain than the catch drawer holds flour. If you pull out the drawer after grinding a full hopper, some of the flour will be pushed behind the drawer and require cleaning before the next grinding. But with repeated use one learns to avoid this petty annoyance by not quite filling the hopper.

The manufacturer warns that corn cannot be milled in the smaller model, but that the larger hawo's is suitable for grinding corn. With the flint corn that I prefer for most of my cornmeal needs, I found that the feed hole on the hopper of the large model would often clog, stopping the milling process. The mill was not damaged, but the annoyance of having to clear the hole with a chopstick (after switching off the mill) nearly every time I wanted to make cornbread or polenta, keeps me from recommending this mill to people whose primary milled grain is corn.

Making the Choice

If you're interested only in flour from wheat and other small grains, most of the electric mills will do this basic task. However, if you bake your own bread and want fresh ground flour, the slowest mills would be out of the question for any except those with greater patience than I. The Jupiter stone mill is too slow and too hot for most practical uses, even for someone who uses only a few cups of flour on occasion. Equipped with the stainless steel grinding head, however, the Jupiter is a good choice for someone who uses small amounts of flour and wants a mill that also will provide cracked grains. And twenty minutes really isn't all that long to wait for enough flour to make a small batch of bread.

The Samap F-50 is the best-performing small-grain-only mill. It's cool-grinding, uses natural grinding surfaces, and is sturdy and reliable. It's also more than quick enough for home flour production.

While the noise and basic construction are enough to make me shy away from the two micronizers, they do grind fine flour quickly. If I had to choose between the two I'd take the Magic Mill III Plus.

I can't recommend the finicky Kootenay A-200 as a home mill, but I must admit to a certain lingering infatuation. When it comes to performance, the Samap F-100 is hard to beat. It has proven reliability, grinds good flour from virtually any grain, and generates little heat. If you grind a lot of corn, the narrow feed opening might be a source of continuing frustration.

The hawo's mills grind all small grains with ease, and with a little adjustment mill a lovely Irish-style stone-ground oatmeal from whole oat groats. It says something of the quality of the mills that my neighbors, who used one of the mills regularly during the month-long testing period, purchased the large hawo's.

With its wooden housing and natural stones, the Kootenay A-130 comes closest to satisfying my aesthetic needs. It also grinds satisfactory flour from all grains except the hardest flint corn, and even that was usable. It is simple to operate, fast, and relatively cool-grinding. With a retail price of around $650 (depending on the currency exchange rate) it's not inexpensive, but there are more expensive mills.

The Meadows outperformed them all as a household mill. It's fast, grinds all grains to flour or meal, uses natural stones, and is built to provide years of service. However, it would be out of place in most

ELECTRIC MILLS

	Milling Surface	Time to Mill 2½ lbs. Bread Flour	Temp. Rise in Flour	Suitable for Cornmeal	Ease of Cleaning 0-5 (easy)	Price
JUPITER STEEL	Stainless steel	17:45	23°	No	4	$269.95
JUPITER STONE	Cast stone	37:30	40° (1)	No	4	224.95
KITCHEN MILL	Stainless steel	4:15	37°	Yes	2	259.95
KOOTENAY A-130	Natural stone	3:40	15°	Yes (coarse only with hard flint corn)	4	650. plus shpg.
KOOTENAY A-200	Natural stone	3:55	8° (2)	Coarse only	0	800. plus shpg.
MAGIC MILL	Stainless steel	1:20	43°	Yes	2	299.
MEADOWS HOUSEHOLD	Natural stone	1:55	16°	Yes	1	670. plus shpg.
SAMAP F-50	Cast stone	7:30	12° (3)	No	3	579.
SAMAP F-100	Cast stone	3:40	15°	With attention	3	739.
HAWO'S Sm	Cast stone	6:40	27°	No	3	454. incl. shpg.
HAWO'S Lg	Cast stone	5:10	27°	With attention	3	598. incl. shpg.

(1) In grinding one pound, (2) After grinding 5 pounds, (3) In grinding one pound; follow-up showed only 3°- 4° additional increase with continuous grinding

home kitchens, looking like the industrial machine that it performs like, and taking up more room than most of us have to spare. For joint family or community use, or even for a small store or bakery, the Meadows could be a good choice.

HAND MILLS

Unless you use a lot of flour or are physically impaired, a hand mill may be a better choice than an electric mill. With the best of the hand mills I was able to reduce 2½ pounds of hard spring wheat to fine flour in only ten minutes. While that may not be as quick as most of the electric mills, it is considerably better than a few of them. None of the hand mills increased the temperature of the flour more than a negligible few degrees, all were quiet to operate, and their use does not feed the nuclear economy. Instead of spending time and money on an exercise class, why not grind your own flour with your own power, fueled by calories from your last batch of home-baked bread?

Because rate of grinding in these manual mills is largely influenced by the person grinding, I'm not including specific times as I did with the electric mills. Rather, I'll use relative terms about ease and speed of operation.

Stone Miller

Made by the Phoenix Foundry in Marcus, Washington, the Stone Miller looks like a relic from the century past. Its massive body is

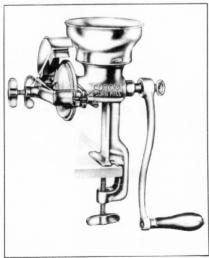

Left: The Corona is inexpensive and grinds both wet and dry material. Above: The Samap has a unique grinding surface that produces fine flour.

made entirely of cast iron and painted black. The crank is mounted at the rim of a large flywheel. An exposed gear reduction system adds to its early-industrial-age ambience. The stones in the Stone Miller, however, are not of that era, but are of the same human-made materials as are those of the Corona stones.

The mill was the worst performer of the few hand mills tested. The reduction gears served their purpose in allowing for easy turning, but the rate of production was painfully slow. Several minutes of grinding produced only a very scant cup of flour. Backing off the adjustment resulted in quicker production, but the result was a mixture of cracked wheat, coarse meal, and fine flour. The crank handle itself is located twelve inches from the center of the flywheel. While I'm sure that this was intended to give a greater advantage through leverage, I found the resulting two-foot diameter too large for comfortable grinding. The reduction gears and long cranking radius are novel ideas, but it seems that the designers could have done more practical testing before implementing them. The mill must be bolted to a sturdy bench or table.

Samap Hand Mill

This unique mill is reminiscent of the stone querns of old, once common in households throughout the civilized world. The entire mill body is cast of a smooth, stonelike material. The Samap comes with its own clamps and can be mounted on a sturdy counter with a 3-inch or larger overhang. This mill is the only hand mill that operates in a horizontal, rather than vertical, plane. I find the grinding motion pleasant and comfortable, but no more so than any of the better-made vertical hand mills. The stones run on steel needle bearings and rotate smoothly. The grinding surfaces are of the same cast natural conglomerate as is used in the Samap electric mills. The mill produces powdery-fine flour and can be adjusted to make coarse flour and even oatflakes.

The Samap hand mill has three shortcomings. The hopper is very small, and its opening is obstructed by the steel handle that runs across its mouth. The flour is discharged into a moat-like trough around the mill stone and must be pushed or brushed into a bowl, adding a step that none of the other mills has. Though the flour may be of excellent texture, if you bake much bread, be warned that you may spend as much time grinding as you do eating.

Diamant Grain Mill

The massive cast-iron, Danish-made Diamant domestic grain mill, at 55 pounds, is the heaviest of all the hand mills. It comes with steel plates or optional stone plates. Like the Country Living and

HAND MILLS

	Milling Surface	Price
CORONA		
STANDARD	Steel	$35.95 postpaid
Fine Plates	Steel	14.95(plates only)
Stone	Synthetic stone	49.95
KING CONVERTIBLE MODEL	Steel/synthetic stone	65.95 with stones and large hopper
COUNTRY LIVING	Hardened cast iron	269.95 plus shpg.
DIAMANT	Steel	350. plus 5% shpg.
Extra plates	Steel	35.
Stones	Cast stone	90.
SAMAP	Cast stone	195.
STONE MILLER	Synthetic stone	249.50 plus shpg.

Phoenix mills, it comes equipped with a grooved flywheel for conversion to either motor or pedal power, and like the Country Living mill it will produce fine flour at a good rate. For extra cost it is available with a variety of steel grinding plates and a set of cast natural conglomerate stones. Equipped with either the fine steel plates or the stones, the Diamant produces pastry-fine flour. Other steel grinding plates produce coarse meal and "kibbled" or cracked grains. When fitted with the steel plates it can be used for grinding wet or oily materials. Regardless of the plate being used, the Diamant is easily adjustable within a wide range of textures.

Partly responsible for the Diamant's high production and ease of use are teeth on the auger that feed the grain from the hopper into the grinding plates. These pre-crack the grain so that the plates are only grinding the already broken kernels, not breaking down whole grains as in other mills.

Although the Diamant disassembles quite easily for thorough cleaning, it is not as self-cleaning as the Country Living mill. The mill is shipped with a coat of metallic green paint with gold trim. The green paint was applied to the entire outside surface of the mill, including the threads on the adjusting screw on the front of the mill. When this is turned, paint will fall into the flour receptacle. This is easily remedied by cleaning the threads before using the mill.

Operated with a motor at the recommended rpm, the Diamant takes six or seven minutes to grind 2½ pounds of spring wheat into fine flour when fitted with the steel plates. Using the stones, the mill, when powered, was slower (nine minutes) and generated more heat. Unless you're committed to stone-ground flour (and to spending an additional $50), the steel plates seem to be a more satisfactory choice.

Corona Mill

This is the old standby: sturdy, inexpensive, and with its steel burrs, versatile. I bought mine in 1971 for twelve dollars (it costs more than twice that now), and it has since seen use not only as a home flour mill, but has ground cooked whole corn for making *masa*, soaked soybeans for tofu, and cooked soybeans for making miso.

As a flour mill it isn't the best. I run the grain through at least twice and often three times to get a rather gritty bread flour. When I first got the mill I would grind five pounds of wheat in about twenty minutes, but production has slowed since then (because I've slowed down, not the mill). Grinding dry, hard grain in a standard Corona is no easy task, but can be made easier if you trickle the grain into the hopper, just a little at a time, as you grind.

Built in Colombia, the Corona is meant to be a masa mill, and at that job it excels, as it does as a soaked soybean mill and as a grinder for any wet or oily product. Synthetic stones are available for the Corona, and with these fine flour is produced, albeit very slowly. Specially cut steel burrs for fine grinding are also available at reasonable cost, although I haven't used these. It is also available with an extra large hopper. The Corona can be clamped to any sturdy table or countertop, providing it has an overhang. You protect the countertop with strips of thin wood. Considering the Corona's low cost, rustic utility, and versatility, there's probably nowhere you can get more mill for your money, but if it's fine flour that you're interested in, this mill may not satisfy you.

Country Living Grain Mill

This U.S.-made, steel-plated mill grinds flour as fine as any stone mill, is as easy as any of the hand mills to crank, and with continuous grinding will produce 2½ pounds of fine flour in eight to ten minutes. The flywheel has a groove for V-belt operation, powered either by electric motor or exercise bicycle (the latter is offered by the manufacturer). The mill has simple lines, is decorated with a cast stalk of grain, and is painted in contrasting beige and brown enamel. The sample that I tested had been in use for two years, and showed no chips in the paint or other signs of wear.

The Country Living Mill will grind all grains, large or small, hard or soft, into flour varying from fine to coarse grits. The manufacturer also recommends it for making soybean grits and for shelling sunflower seeds. Overall, it's a versatile, efficient, quality mill.

Making the Choice

If your only interest in owning a grain mill is to produce flour from small grains like wheat, rye, and barley, you've a wider choice than someone who also wants to grind cornmeal and wet material. Since none of the electric mills can grind soaked soybeans for making tofu or cooked corn for making masa, the Corona would be the ideal mill for that purpose and for limited grain grinding. Given the low cost of this mill, and the fact that it is ideally suited for wet grinding, I would choose to use the Corona for these purposes and have a second mill for grinding dry grains into flour, meal, and cracked grain for morning cereals.

The Stone Miller is attractive and the designers had some good ideas. However, the poor execution of these concepts, and the resultant poor performance of the mill, make this mill little more than a conversation piece. The Samap, though it does grind beautiful flour on natural surfaces, is too slow for anything but an occasional cup or two of flour; it's not a tool for the serious baker. Of the hand mills I tested it's a choice between the Diamant and the Country Living Grain Mill. Either one will cost as much as some of the electric mills. The Diamant is more expensive and more versatile. The Country Living is more compact and a little easier to crank owing to the main shaft running on sealed bearings rather than just in lubricated sleeves. Both are convertible to other sources of power, and the Country Living Grain Mill is available from the manufacturer as a combination exercise bicycle and grain mill.

RESOURCES

Corona Mill: R & R Mill Company
48 West First North
Smithfield, UT 84335

Country Living Mill: Country Living Products
14727 56th Ave. NW
Stanwood, WA 98292

Diamant Domestic Grain Mill: In-Tec Equipment Company
Box 123
D.V. Station
Dayton, OH 45406
or
Oven Crafters
P.O. Box 24
Tomales, CA 94971

Hawo's: hawo's Flour Mills
P.O. Box 24
Salmon Arm, British Columbia V1E 4N3 Canada

Jupiter Mills: Miracle Exclusives
P.O. Box 349
Locust Valley, NY 11560

Kitchenetics, the manufacturer of the Kitchen Mill, appears to have gone out of business since our test. Information on this mill is included as there are some still in operation or available used.

Kootenay Mills: Kootenay Natural Stone Mills
P.O. Box 1084
Kaslo, British Columbia V0G 1M0 Canada

Magic Mill III Plus: Magic Mill
1911 South 3850 West
Salt Lake City, UT 84104

Meadows Household Mill: Meadows Mill Company
P.O. Box 1288
North Wilkesboro, NC 28659

Samap Mills: Miracle Exclusives
P.O. Box 349
Locust Valley, NY 11560
or
Grain and Salt Society
14351 Wycliff Way
P.O. Box DD
Magalia, CA 95954

Stone Miller: Phoenix Foundry
Box 68
Marcus, WA 99151

BAKING WITH NATURAL LEAVENING

T
HE METHOD DESCRIBED IN THIS BOOK IS BUT ONE OF MANY TO MAKE NATURALLY LEAVENED BREAD. THERE ARE AS MANY VARIATIONS AS there are bakers, and all will yield good bread. When I visited master baker Richard Bourdon, a baker of *natur-desembrod* for five years in Amsterdam and now of the Berkshire Mountain Bakery, at his western Massachusetts home, he explained these many variations, all yielding very similar bread: "What any baker does is to create the proper balance between the expansive and contractive forces at play in the bread and in the universe. If a method uses significantly less sourdough [leaven] than another, the baker will either use more of another expansive element or less of a contractive one."

The leaven is obviously an expansive element in baking, as are warm water, warm proofing temperatures, and long proofing times. Salt strengthens gluten and slows fermentation, so it plays a contractive role in the baking process. A soft (slack) dough will expand more readily than a drier, stiff one. Unkneaded, wet pancake batter will spread flat when poured out of a bowl. An overkneaded, stiff dough made without leavening, will sit for days and not sag a fraction (nor rise!).

Gluten, the primary protein in wheat, responds to certain elements in much the same way as do our muscles, the primary proteins in the body. Take a plunge in an icy mountain stream and your body tightens. Soak in a hot spring and it unwinds. Work your muscles hard, without stopping to relax, and you'll increase your chances of pulling one. Cold water tightens gluten and slows fermentation. Overworked dough will tighten and not be able to relax and rise fully. And unless it is allowed to rest between each working or kneading, dough will tear instead of stretch.

Understanding the interplay between these contractive and expansive elements can help you adapt your baking to seasonal changes. In warm weather you might choose to use colder water, a little less leaven, or a little more salt. If your leaven isn't as strong as usual you may not only use a little more of it but also decrease some of the contractive elements, perhaps by using warmer water and a little less salt.

What is true for the bread is true for the leaven. If your bread isn't rising properly and the dough seems a little sluggish, your leaven is probably weak. Make it slightly stiffer, with cooler water, and store it at lower temperatures for a few bakes. It seems to gain strength through adversity. By working against stiff dough and low temperatures the leaven actually seems to grow in power. Your rejuvenated leaven will make more delicious and lighter bread.

Here's the rule of thumb: the potential strength of your dough is inversely proportional to the amount of leaven. The less leaven you can use and still get good bread, the better the bread will be. Now don't take this to be a license to decrease the leaven to a tablespoon per two-loaf batch, but do strive to reduce the amount of leaven in the recipe as your leaven grows in strength. The two cup amount called for in the recipes to follow is for a fairly young, but strong, leaven that has been maintained properly. An older leaven is not necessarily stronger, and can, in fact, be much weaker than one in the freshness of youth. If you use the leaven frequently, twice a week or more, keep it cool at all times, use good water and fresh flour, and don't make it too slack. Take good care of your leaven and it will continue to increase in leavening power and you will find your dough ripening in less time than before. If you do not treat your leaven to the ideal life, it will not get stronger as it ages and will even weaken.

Let's assume you have been a faithful leaven keeper but your bread still isn't behaving properly. When you check your dough after only two hours you are surprised to find that it has risen dramatically in the bowl. And after you shape the loaves you find that they also rise more quickly than you expect. But when you place them on the hearth they sink and spread, rather than rise. The crumb of the finished bread is of reasonable texture, but the loaf is flat. The problem is probably too much leaven. (Unless you've changed the wheat or flour.)

You may think that a solution to this problem would be to shape the loaves earlier and to reduce the total proofing time. This might help, as might using colder water, cooler proofing temperatures, and more salt. But the problem of too much leaven isn't simply one of too much of an expansive element that can be corrected by increasing the contractive elements. Sometimes excess is excess, and the best way to restore balance is to get rid of the surplus rather than add something else.

Ripe leaven has virtually no stretch because the organisms have "digested" the gluten; it contributes little to the physical structure of the bread, but it does contribute weight that needs to be lifted if the loaf is to be light. The less there is to lift, the lighter the bread (as long as your leaven is strong enough to provide adequate lift in the first place). But don't go to extremes to use less leaven. Don't push up the dough temperatures or cut back on the salt just to reduce the amount of leaven in your recipe. Relatively cool dough temperatures and a proper measure of salt are important for good bread, and the purpose of all this, after all, is to make good bread. If the basic formula that is recommended here has worked well for you, but in subsequent bakings you begin to observe the above too-much-leaven symptoms, then it's time to consider using less.

How much less? After repeated weak, but active, doughs, I cut the amount of leaven by half. Seems dramatic, but it works. You may want to gradually reduce the leaven quantity until your bread improves. Be sure to increase the flour, water, and salt to make up for the loss of dough volume by decreasing the leaven by one cup.

The too-much-leaven symptoms often appear when the weather warms unexpectedly, and almost always as winter gives way to spring and spring to summer. If you run into a short warm spell you can just use slightly cooler water until the chill returns. With a change of seasons, however, decrease the leaven and gradually lower temperatures as the season progresses. You'll probably have to reverse the process in the fall.

If you want to make larger quantities of bread per batch, decrease the proportion of leaven as dough weight increases. If your dough weighs forty pounds or more, 10 percent or less of the total should be leaven, assuming your leaven is strong.

One can bake good bread occasionally (or even often) by formula, but if you understand the principles behind the process you will know when to change the elements within your formula in order to make consistently better bread. And when you experience the bewilderment that accompanies bread making failures, at least you'll have the satisfaction of understanding the process.

THE SECRETS OF
BETTER BREAD BAKING

THE WARMTH OF THE MASSIVE BRICK OVEN AND THE SMELLS OF WOODSMOKE AND FRESHLY BAKED BREAD WERE A WELCOME CHANGE from the cold rain and the low-lying clouds that shrouded the Eiffel Tower. But more than inclement weather had driven me to this ancient room beneath the Boulevard de Grenelle. Rumor of the excellence of the bread had reached me halfway around the world. The Poilane family's bakeries in Paris make what has become the standard by which all other breads in France are judged. So far, none has surpassed the hearty hearth-baked loaves that come from their wood-fired ovens beneath Boulevard de Grenelle or the original Poilane bakery on Rue de Cherche-Midi.

Poilane's bakers make thousands of huge, two-kilo loaves from bolted (sifted) stone-ground French wheat flour, fermented with *levain*, and baked on the hearths of the wood-fired ovens. Their most popular bread is at least a foot in diameter and has a chewy, dark, flour-dusted crust. The rustic loaves seem more fitting for a French farmhouse of the last century than a bakery in the heart of sophisticated Paris.

The levain used in the fermentation and raising of Poilane's country-style loaves is known as *desem* in Flemish and Dutch and variously as sourdough and leaven in English. In the mid-1970s, Paul Petrofsky and Hy Lerner established Baldwin Hill Bakery, one of the first of the new generation of natural leaven bakeries in this country. Today Lerner is still at the helm of Baldwin Hill and the wood-fired

49

oven turns out over 10,000 hearth-baked loaves every week.

Chuck and Carla Conway's O'Bread Bakery in the Champlain Valley of Shelburne, Vermont, uses a method derived from the same Belgian bakery that inspired Baldwin Hill. After a visit to France, Helen and Jules Raben began baking *pain au levain* in a stone and brick oven they built behind their house in rural Plainfield, Vermont. Their efforts, and those of other bread making pioneers such as the Ponce French Bakery in Chico, California, are quietly turning the wheels of a bread revolution in this country.

Many of these bakeries have their own unique processes, and each bread is distinct. But the externals of these breads are similar. All are made with stone-ground wheat and are baked on the brick hearth of the oven; some fire their ovens with wood.

The large loaf of Poilane that I bought in Paris became my new standard of perfection in bread. Soon thereafter, I began trying to replicate a whole wheat version of it in my home. In addition to visiting bakeries, I learned much from *The Laurel's Kitchen Bread Book* and yet more from Berkshire Mountain baker Richard Bourdon. I am indebted to them for the guide to making naturally leavened bread that follows.

We can each have our own stone mill and buy—or even grow— wheat of good baking quality. The leaven can be made as readily at home as in a bakery. But how does one create the special atmosphere of a brick oven in one's home? In her *English Breads and Yeast Cookery*, Elizabeth David describes the portable clay ovens once used in parts of Britain. Inspired by these, David suggested covering baking loaves—within a kitchen oven—with an inverted, large ceramic bowl. The method works tolerably well, yielding loaves with a robust, chewy crust. The dome of the inverted bowl contains the steam of the baking bread, allowing the slow development of the crust; it mimics the shape of a traditional beehive oven and captures the convected heat of a gas or electric range and transforms it into radiant heat.

The bowl method does have its drawbacks. The heat was gradually discoloring my mother-in-law's favorite mixing bowl, and the bowl itself was a bit hard to handle at 500° F.

Baking in a terra cotta "chicken roaster" worked as well as the inverted bowl, and the roaster was much easier to handle. Covered Pyrex pots proved equally as satisfactory, but the loaves just weren't the same as a large round loaf, baked directly on the hearth.

There is now available a kitchen gadget that flawlessly recreates a true brick-oven atmosphere within the oven of a standard range. The loaves I bake in my stoneware cooking bell or *cloche* are virtually indistinguishable from those loaves baked in a brick oven; the only thing missing is the woodsmoke. The domed lid has a convenient handle. If the lid is soaked for a few minutes before baking, it creates just the right amount of steam around the baking loaf. (Cooking bells are available in many kitchenware shops and from some gourmet kitchenware catalogs.)

The main purpose of any of these "oven inserts" is the same: to create a steamy environment in which the loaves will bake by radiant heat as they do within a brick oven. In effect, they are ovens within ovens.

The only other special paraphernalia that I use are cloth-lined baskets or bowls for proofing, or rising the loaves. For one large hearth loaf from the recipe that follows, I use a basket about nine inches in diameter with a cotton liner stitched to it. For two smaller loaves, I use seven-inch baskets. Bowls with cloth liners work just as well.

GETTING STARTER STARTED

There are three ways to acquire a starter for your naturally leavened bread. The first two, buying it or obtaining it from a friend, are the easiest. Several companies offer dried sourdough starter and it is available both in stores and through the mail. GEM Cultures of Fort Bragg, California, also offers a "living sourdough culture." A small jar of thin batter will appear on your doorstep a few days after you order. The contents, combined with whole wheat flour and water, and used as below, worked well for me.

If a friend is already making good naturally leavened bread, perhaps he or she will give you a few ounces of dough. Maintained according to the guidelines that follow, any reasonably good starter would prove satisfactory and be able to leaven bread indefinitely. If you are starting from a store-bought starter or from a friend's that has been kept as a batter, first make a batter as per their instructions. When that batter is obviously active and frothy, mix in enough flour to make a fairly stiff dough. You should have enough to make a ball about the size of a tennis ball. Knead until smooth, shape into a ball, and wrap as described below, under "Keeping the Culture Going."

There are problems with both of the above methods. First, you may one day accidentally "lose" your starter. If your friend or commercial source is no longer available—alas, no leaven! Secondly, most sourdough sold and used in this country is of the San Francisco or Alaska type. This is usually maintained as a batter or very soft dough at relatively warm temperatures. The balance of organisms present is suited to that environment. The starter is quite sharp and sour-tasting, flavors that get in the way of the wheat. Although cooler temperatures and stiffer dough will effect a shift toward a more "fruity" fermentation, why undo something that's already been done?

However, you can bypass these problems by making your own natural leaven, using only freshly ground whole wheat flour and unchlorinated water. The result will be a culture that is adapted to the conditions under which it will spend its life. Ideally, a starter will have its origin and spend its formative years in an environment not unlike that in which it will live and work.

Omer Gevaert, the founder of the Belgian bakery that inspired Baldwin Hill Bakery, recommends starting a leaven from a ball of dough buried in a bag of flour, hidden away in the cool of a deciduous forest. I've had success with his basic method, without the forest, though the cool is essential. *The Laurel's Kitchen Bread Book* describes this process in detail, but the basics can be conveyed more briefly.

Using organically grown, freshly ground whole wheat flour and cool spring water, make a fairly stiff dough about the size of a tennis ball. Bury this ball in the center of a ten-pound bag of the same flour and keep in a cool place (50° to 65°F). After two days, remove the ball. Discard half the dough and the skin that has formed around the ball. Soften the remaining dough in more spring water and add enough flour to make another ball the same size as the first. Bury it in the flour again. Repeat this process on each of the next two days. Then remove the ball from the flour bag and soften the entire ball in one-third of a cup of water. Add enough flour to make a dough and knead until smooth. Leave at the same temperature for another day, but now in a covered ceramic or glass container. After twenty-four hours, soften in another one-third cup of water, add more flour, knead, and leave again for twenty-four hours.

From this point on, the culture can be maintained as described below, but for the next week, keep the temperature below 65°F and replenish daily by making a new starter ball and new leaven on alternate days. Although the leaven is not yet up to full strength, you may bake with it at any point.

At first the ball of dough will smell only like freshly milled wheat. By the end of the first week it should have developed a sweet fragrance, much like the smell of sprouting wheat. Midway through the second week, your starter will have begun to develop its own distinctive nose, influenced by the wheat itself, and the organisms that were on the grain when it was milled. Other instructions for making starter from scratch often start with soured noodle water, sour grain, milk, potatoes, or even yeast. Others suggest making a batter and letting it catch "wild yeast spores." Because this starter is made from only flour and water, and because it is nurtured in a closed environment, surrounded only by more flour, it contains only what naturally occurred on and in the wheat. Like good wine that is a product of the vineyard, fermented only by the indigenous organisms from the skin of the fruit, bread from this starter is truly a product of the wheat and of the earth from which it sprang.

THE LEAVEN

Once you have made your starter and it has come up to strength you are ready to begin bread making. There are three basic steps and three corresponding doughs. The *starter* is the seed culture for making the *leaven*, which is in turn seed for both the *final bread dough* and the next starter.

The starter and the leaven contain only flour and water, no salt or any other extraneous ingredients. Salt, which strengthens gluten, inhibits fermentation and is generally a contractive element in the baking process. It would serve only to weaken the leavening power of the ferment and to slow down its action, as any gluten is digested by the starter organisms. Also, for the starter or the leaven, the use of a high-gluten spring wheat would be counter-productive; I generally use hard red winter wheat (lower in gluten than spring wheat) and have had success with lower-gluten pastry flour made from soft wheat.

While the bread dough itself does not normally play a part in the cycle of regeneration, it can, in an emergency, be used to continue the culture. If you should discover that you have forgotten to make a new starter from the leaven when you made your final dough, all is not lost. Pinch or snip a small piece of the dough anytime before you bake it, but ideally before you shape your loaves. Combine this with flour and water to make a small leaven, and make this leaven into a new starter ball and continue as usual. The small amount of salt in the dough may at first diminish the leavening power but it will soon be back to normal.

In the leaven, you take the concentrated leavening power of the starter and increase it to a volume approximately one-third the size of your final dough. Here the organisms inside the compact starter ball find elbow room and ample food to multiply and flourish.

Because the starter begets the leaven which begets the starter, it's difficult to decide which process to describe first. It's the same philosophical dilemma that has been confounding the French *boulanger* for generations: What came first, the *chef* or the *levain*? (Chef is the French baker's term for the starter culture.) Once your leavening culture is established, you will always begin your baking cycle by making a leaven, so we will begin there.

To make this leaven, remove the outer cloth from the starter ball and carefully unwrap the inner cloth. The starter ball should be covered with a dusting of flour and be encased in a firm "rind." Break the ball in half and peel the rind from the outside. The ripe starter should be well aerated and have a pleasant, fresh aroma, fruity with a hint of grape or peach, and only slightly sour. The gluten should be completely digested so the starter has no "stretch" left to it. Dissolve the soft starter in three-quarters of a cup of cool water, breaking up any lumps with your fingers. To this milky liquid add two cups of flour and mix thoroughly. Knead for several minutes, adding either flour or water if necessary to form a stiff dough.

Form a sphere with the kneaded dough and place in a ceramic bowl or glass jar with twice the volume as the dough. Cover with a damp towel, sheet of plastic, or, if using a jar, loosely screw or set on the lid. Place the container in a spot with a temperature between 60° and 70° F.

The leaven will be ready to use in no less than fourteen hours and should be used within twenty-four hours. Ideally, the leaven will have doubled in volume, its interior should lack the elastic quality of gluten, and it should have a pleasant, distinctly fruity aroma, much like the starter from which it was made.

KEEPING THE CULTURE GOING

From the mature leaven, take the portion that you don't use to make your batch of bread (a little less than a cup), knead a handful of flour into it, round it, and wrap as follows. You'll need two clean, dry cotton or linen cloths, about fifteen inches square. One of these, at least, must be undyed. (Fifteen-inch-square handkerchiefs work fine.)

Spread an undyed cloth on the counter. Four inches from the top edge and halfway between the two sides, place a few tablespoons of flour. Place the rounded dough on top of the flour and put a few more spoonfuls of flour on top of the ball. Some of this will fall around the sides. Don't fret, that's exactly what you want! This flour will keep the dough from sticking to the cloth and will help to form the starter's protective rind.

Next, fold the top edge of the cloth over the top of the ball. If you've placed the ball properly, this flap should just half cover the ball. Fold one side over the ball, then the other. Fold the remaining flap over the top and turn the ball over. Grasp the end of this last flap with your right hand, hold the ball with your left, and pull the cloth snug. Hold the tension and wrap any remaining cloth, taking care not to deform the ball excessively.

Position the wrapped ball on the second cloth in the same position as you placed the rounded dough on the first. With the outer cloth you will wrap the ball at a right angle to the first wrap. Wrap in the same manner as with the first cloth. Pull the cloth as snug as you

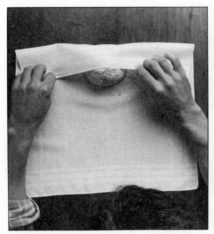

STARTER WRAPPING
Place the unripened starter on the floured cloth, fold the cloth around the ball, and wrap tightly. Repeat with a second cloth.

can get it. Secure the outer cloth with an elastic or piece of string, or place it with the last flap down to prevent the cloth from unwrapping as the starter expands.

The wrapped starter should be kept at cool room temperature (60° to 70° F) if you plan to begin another batch of bread the next day, or put in the refrigerator if you won't be baking for several days or a week. As the starter ripens, it will stretch against the cloths. If you've folded well, the ball will inflate from the gases of fermentation and blow the package up like an overstuffed pillow. The ball should be hard and the cloth as taut as a drumhead. If the ball is soft, and the top sunken rather than tightly arched, the starter was too warm, left for too long, or wrapped loosely. It will probably still make good bread, but try to correct the problem the next time. Make the leaven earlier, put the ball in the refrigerator for a few hours to retard its development, or fold more carefully.

If you have kept your starter ball in the refrigerator for a few days, remove it several hours before you plan to make your next leaven. This allows it to warm to cool room temperature and regain activity. The starter must be used or reactivated at least once a week, and ideally twice.

MAKING THE DOUGH

I usually make one or two large loaves of bread, reminiscent of those wonderful loaves of Poilane. This recipe is for one of those or two smaller loaves.

Approximately 2 cups ripe leaven
5½ cups whole wheat bread flour
2 cups cool spring (or other unchlorinated) water
½ - 1½ teaspoons salt

Freshly milled, moderately coarse flour containing flakes of bran seems to work better than very finely and uniformly ground flour. While the latter will make a fine-textured, light bread, the dough can be quite sticky and difficult to handle without adding flour as you knead. I usually use hard red winter wheat, but you can use hard spring wheat with good results. A blend of winter and spring wheats will give the bread the benefit of the flavor of the winter and the higher gluten content of the spring. I nearly always mill my flour the day I use it, often only moments before I begin mixing.

In a large mixing bowl dissolve 1½ cups of the leaven in two cups of water. Make a new starter ball with the remaining leaven. Add the flour to the water and leaven mix.

If you've made bread before, you've probably first mixed the ingredients with a wooden spoon and then, once the ingredients began to come together, removed them to a floured board for kneading. During kneading you would add flour occasionally to keep the dough from sticking. Let's try something a little different this time. Place a basin of cool water next to your mixing bowl. Use this water to wet your hands as you mix the flour, leaven, and water together. When all the flour is moistened, with one hand start folding the dough toward the center of the bowl. With the other hand rotate the dough a quarter turn for each fold. If the dough begins to stick to your hands, dip them in the basin again and gently shake off the excess water. Mix in this way for two minutes, cover the bowl with a towel and rinse your hands.

A soft dough will be more responsive in the oven and will cook more thoroughly than a stiff dough, so try to keep the dough soft. However, because you will be adding a small amount of water as you knead, start with the dough a little on the stiff side. You can always add water as you knead, but you can't take it out.

Five minutes later, sprinkle the salt over the top of the dough, remoisten your hands, and continue folding the dough as before. This time, after you make the fold, press down firmly with your closed

SHAPING THE LOAF
The dough is flattened, folded, kneaded into a teardrop shape to seal the folds, then rounded.

hand or the heel of your hand in the center of the dough, releasing quickly. Once the dough has come together, *lightly* moisten your countertop or other smooth kneading surface, and turn the dough out onto it. Knead as you were doing in the bowl for 200 strokes. Let the dough rest, covered, for five minutes.

After the five-minute rest, for both you and the dough, knead another 200 strokes, remoistening your hands and the kneading surface as necessary. Cover, and let rest for another five minutes. When you take up the dough again you'll notice that the dough is more elastic than it was after the last kneading. This dough will probably be softer than you are used to. If the dough is too soft and sticks to your wet hands, it probably could use a touch more flour, but don't overdo it. Knead another 200 strokes, then round the dough and place it, smooth side up, in the bowl and cover or insert the bowl with dough into a plastic bag.

Let the dough sit undisturbed for two hours at warm room temperature (70° to 80° F). At the end of two hours, the dough should have begun to rise. Moisten your hands and give the dough a few turns, deflating it to its original volume. Be careful that you don't tear the soft dough. Let the dough sit for another hour and a half.

SHAPING AND PROOFING THE LOAVES

By now the surface of the dough should have lost its shininess and nearly doubled in volume. Deflate it again. After letting it rest for five minutes, turn the dough out onto a lightly floured surface, smooth-side-down. If you are baking two loaves instead of one large loaf, cut the dough into two pieces. First, pre-shape the loaves. Flatten the dough into a large circle about an inch thick. Fold the circle not quite in half. Next, fold in the right side, the bottom, and the left, pressing each side down in the center. Turn the dough on its side and knead the bottom together while turning the dough, making a teardrop shape. When the folds are sealed, set the loaf aside to rest for five minutes, covered, to protect from drafts.

Repeat the above pre-shaping procedure, except for the five-minute rest. Turn the loaf smooth-side-up and round the loaf with a gentle, yet firm, motion.

Dust your cloth-lined proofing basket or bowl with flour and place the rounded loaf smooth-side-down in the basket. Cover the basket with a sheet of plastic or smooth, damp toweling or place in a closed plastic bag. Put the dough in a warm (85° to 90° F) spot for the final proofing which should take about one and a half to two hours. I use my oven, which is kept at just the right temperature by the pilot light. If your oven is not quite warm enough, remedy this by boiling a large pot of water and placing it uncovered at the bottom of the oven. The steam will both warm the oven and provide humidity to prevent a crust from forming on the dough.

Proofing hearth loaves (letting them rise) in baskets has several advantages over proofing them on a flat sheet. The eventual top and sides of the loaf that are in contact with the cloth stay soft and moist, allowing the dough to expand without restriction. What will be the bottom of the loaf is the only exposed part of the loaf as it proofs, and may dry slightly. Instead of creating a problem, as a dry top crust would, this can provide a firm foundation for the loaf as it is loaded onto the hearth of your oven or the base of your baking cloche. A dough that is too soft will hold its shape in a basket, but would spread out like a pancake if unsupported.

If you are proofing your bread in the same container that you will be baking it, place the smooth, seamless side up.

Just before the bread is fully proofed, remove it from the oven and preheat the oven to 500° F if you are baking the bread covered or at 450° F if uncovered. If you are using a baking stone or a tile hearth be sure to preheat it in the oven. If you will be using a cloche, preheat the base. If you are using an unglazed terra cotta or stoneware cloche for your bread, fill the top only with warm water. The bread should now be just less than twice its original size, fully aerated, yet still able to spring back if gently probed with the back of a finger. If the size of your proofing basket is properly matched to your loaf size, the dough should now completely fill the basket and be slightly rounded above the basket level.

It should take about two hours from the time of shaping to the time of baking. This will vary depending upon air, water, and flour temperatures, strength of leaven, and amount of salt in the dough. It is better to bake a slightly under-proofed loaf than an over-proofed one. A loaf that has proofed too long will have little, if any, oven spring (it won't rise further in the oven), it won't recover when probed, and it will have a sour smell. As finished bread, it will have a slightly sharp taste and a crumbly texture.

BAKING THE BREAD

If you're using a stoneware baking bell, lightly dust the top (soon to be the bottom) of the loaf in the basket with coarse flour or corn-meal. Pour the water from the top of the bell. Using heavy oven mitts, invert the preheated base of the bell over the top of the proofed bread, then quickly invert everything, setting the base on a heat-proof tile or mat on the countertop. Remove the basket and cloth with care and quickly make several half-inch deep slashes in the top of the loaf, using either a sharp serrated knife or a single-edged razor blade. These cuts allow steam to escape from the inside of the loaf as it bakes and permit orderly expansion of the loaf during the early stages of baking. Without them the loaf might crack irregularly, or the crust might prevent complete rising in the oven. The slashes can be in several patterns, a simple cross, a tic-tac-toe square, or whatever simple design that appeals to you. A good baker knows how each style of cutting affects the rising and baking of a loaf, and will vary cuts with different qualities of dough. Quickly cover the loaf with the bell and place the bell on a low shelf in your oven.

If you have proofed your bread in the pot you will be baking it in, you have only to slash the loaf and put the cover in place (soaked first if unglazed pottery) and bake.

If you are baking your loaf on a tile hearth or baking stone in your oven, you will need to first transfer the loaf onto a floured peel before putting it in the oven. This peel can be one sold in kitchenware shops for pizza, or you can fashion one yourself out of thin wood or even stiff cardboard. Turn the loaf onto the peel, slash it, and quickly place it on the tiles. To do this, simply position the peel where you want the loaf to rest, and deftly, smoothly, and quickly pull the peel out from under the bread.

If you are baking your loaf uncovered, you will need to introduce steam into the oven. One way of doing this is to place a shallow metal baking pan on the floor of the oven before you pre-heat. When you put your bread in the oven, also pour some hot water onto this pan. Be careful! Steam burns. A safer and more effective approach for me has been to spray the oven and the loaves with water using a houseplant sprayer that you use exclusively for this—liquid seaweed and insecticidal soap don't improve the taste of bread. It's safer to bake in a covered ceramic or ovenproof glass pot, and the bread generally comes out better as well.

After ten minutes lower the oven temperature to 400° to 425°F if the bread is covered. If the bread is not covered, spray with water again and reduce heat to 375° to 400°F. Forty minutes after you put the bread into the oven, remove the bell cover. If the bread is still soft, replace the cover and bake for another ten minutes. If it is hard, leave the cover off, but let the bread bake for an additional five minutes uncovered to develop a darker crust. The ideal crust will be a shiny, rich, golden reddish-brown. When the bread is done, place the loaf on a rack to cool for six hours before slicing.

No cutting into your fresh bread, still warm from the oven? Sounds like sacrilege to the home baker, but the bread really isn't done cooking yet. The very center of the loaf has probably only just now reached the boiling point. To cut the loaf now, letting steam and heat escape, would be like opening a pot of rice before it is done. Sylvester Graham insisted on allowing a loaf to ripen for a full twenty-four hours after baking before it was eaten. Others say that a good loaf of naturally leavened bread doesn't reach its peak until the third or fourth day.

If you can't resist the aroma and taste of warm bread, bake a few small rolls alongside your loaf. Eat these first instead of sacrificing a large loaf before its time.

LIGHTER LOAVES

To produce nearly whole-grain flour, millers of the early nineteenth century would grind wheat and bolt out the coarse part. The coarse portion would be ground and sifted again, and the fine flour from the two siftings blended together. I sometimes do the same thing at home using a very fine brass sieve. The coarse bran that doesn't make it through the second bolting is about 5 percent of the total weight of the wheat. It consists mostly of the outermost bran layer and is primarily cellulose. This is the most indigestible portion of the whole wheat kernel and contains very few nutrients.

The bread I make from this flour is slightly lighter and finer-textured than that made from 100 percent whole wheat flour. In general appearance and flavor it is virtually indistinguishable from its whole-grain counterpart.

Those two-kilo round loaves that have made Poilane's Paris bakeries world-renowned are made with a stone-ground flour that has had the bran sifted out of it, with the germ remaining. The flour is a rich creamy color and retains much of the aroma and flavor of the whole wheat. Research has shown that flour sifted through the proper mesh silk sieve has as much as 60 percent of the thiamine found in the whole wheat berries, while modern, unenriched white flour contains 20 percent or less. Bread made with this flour and my usual whole wheat leaven is as close (but still has a long way to go) to Poilane's as any I've had outside of Paris. The crust is dark and chewy, the inside a creamy beige, and the flavor a complexity of wheat and leaven. Bread made from "unbleached white flour," even when naturally leavened, doesn't even come close.

The only variation I have found necessary in making bread with this flour instead of whole wheat is that I use a little less leaven. The dough, especially if too soft, can be sticky and hard to handle.

My daily bread is still the simplest: freshly milled whole wheat flour, spring water, and a touch of salt, leavened with the simple starter made with only the same flour and water. This is bread worthy of its name, truly the staff of life.

RESOURCES

Baking bells are available from
Williams-Sonoma
P.O. Box 7307
San Francisco, CA 94120-7307
(catalog free) or from quality kitchenware shops.

Dry or fresh sourdough starter is available from
GEM Cultures
30301 Sherwood Road
Fort Bragg, CA 95437
Rye or whole wheat starters available. Write for free catalog.

ADDING SOME SPICE!

MOST BREAD BOOKS HAVE ONE RECIPE FOR SOURDOUGH, DESEM-RISEN, OR NATURALLY LEAVENED BREAD—GENERALLY JUST A BASIC wheaten loaf. Perhaps there will be a sourdough rye, but often that uses baker's yeast for the primary leavening, relying on the starter only for flavor and "conditioning." The yeasted sections have dozens of recipes for oatmeal, sesame, and nut bread; for raisin, Swedish rye, and herb breads; for French loaves, dinner rolls, and cinnamon buns. The inference is that natural leavening is fine for simple, hearty fare, but that if you want variety in your bread box, you'd better stock up on Red Star or some other commercial yeast.

Nonsense. Once you're comfortable with the method of making naturally leavened bread you needn't limit yourself to one recipe for the rest of your life. With the basic method and the understanding of a few baking principles, you can make an infinite variety of breads and never purchase baker's yeast again. Any bread worth the salt in it can be risen with natural leavening.

Except in the rye breads described in the following chapter, it is best to allow wheat to be the background for other ingredients in your bread. In adapting the basic recipe in the preceding chapter, substitute one cup, at the very most two, of non-wheaten flour or meal for an equivalent portion of the 5½ cups of whole wheat flour. I add seeds, nuts, and reconstituted dried fruits at the last possible moment, usually after dividing the dough and before shaping. I generally avoid adding sweeteners to bread, but it can be done if you use a light hand.

The sugars *will* affect the fermentation and may enter into the process, possibly contributing off-flavors to the bread. A small amount of oil can be added when you mix the dough. Remember to use only whole wheat flour and non-chlorinated water in the leaven and always be sure that you have set aside and fed the starter before adding other ingredients.

Substituting ingredients is one way to introduce variety in your baking. Another is to make different breads from the basic dough by altering size, shape, proofing time, baking method, and temperature. English muffins, breadsticks, and assorted rolls are all possibilities. Pita is probably the easiest of all breads to make well consistently, and seems an entirely different food than a two-pound hearth loaf made of the same dough baked in the same oven.

I am including here only a few recipes for some of my favorite leavened variations. Let your creativity guide you toward adapting your favorite yeast breads and developing your own new varieties. Do keep it simple. Too many ingredients tend to confuse the taste. Let each variety be distinctly itself. If you use sesame seeds in the dough, toast them first and use enough to make the bread definitely sesame, perhaps a ½ cup per loaf. Walnut bread? Nutty's the word.

PAIN AUX NOIX

Literally bread with nuts, and nuts to the French are walnuts. There are so many in this bread that it might be more accurate to call it Noix aux Pain. While I hesitate to say any bread is my favorite, this is my choice for special occasions, and perhaps would be regular fare if I had a walnut tree in the garden. The pigment in the walnut skin colors the entire crumb a rich reddish-brown, and the slice is studded with irregular cream-colored nut sections. Small round loaves with four parallel cuts are traditional, and bake more thoroughly than large loaves or pan breads. I cut three loaves instead of my usual two. Nuts protrude everywhere.

1 recipe of basic leavened bread
3½ cups walnut halves, chopped

The dough for this is identical to the basic naturally leavened whole wheat dough of the previous chapter, although it is easier to incorporate the nuts if the dough is a little slack. I buy unbroken walnut halves and chop them into half-inch pieces just before making the bread. Add the nuts when you divide the dough to shape the loaves, working the nuts into each loaf separately. Round the loaves, let them rest, and round again for the final shaping. Be careful not to proof this bread too long as the extra weight of the walnuts will make the loaf flat and dense. If in doubt, bake it early. Cook as described in the previous chapter, but decrease the temperature to 400°F, and lower it to 375°F fifteen minutes into the bake. Pain aux Noix may take an extra quarter-hour to bake.

CHRISTMAS MORNING MAPLE-CINNAMON LOAF

Less work than cinnamon rolls and easily as delectable. I make a full recipe of dough, use half for this breakfast bread and reserve the other for a light loaf for dinner.

2 cups leaven
2 cups water
5½ cups sifted (coarse bran removed) whole wheat flour or
*   3 cups whole wheat flour and 2½ cups unbleached flour*
salt
corn, sesame oil, or melted butter
maple syrup
cinnamon

Before retiring Christmas Eve, mix the dough in the usual way, using the above flour instead of all whole wheat. Like walnut bread, this will come out better if the dough is slack. Cover the bowl and store overnight in a cool place—less than 50°F would be ideal. The next day, about one-half hour before dividing, warm the dough to room temperature. You can also mix the dough right after supper and let it sit for a few hours at room temperature. Then put it in the refrigerator before going to bed. Take it out three hours before you intend to bake and let it warm to room temperature for about one hour before dividing.

Divide the dough into halves. On a floured board roll half the dough into a ½-inch-thick rectangle. Liberally brush the top first with oil, then with maple syrup. Sprinkle with cinnamon, roll into cylinder, and coil into a 2-quart covered casserole. Let proof, then bake, covered, for 45 minutes at 375°F. Uncover and bake for another 10 minutes to brown, if necessary. Serve while still warm. If your dough was especially soft, the coil will have melded into a round loaf and the syrup, oil, and cinnamon will be streaked across every slice. I shape and bake the other half of the dough as a hearth loaf to have with Christmas dinner. But of course you can make two Christmas morning loaves (and eat more stuffing with your dinner).

PITA

After having made hundreds of successful pocket breads I am

still awed by the oven's magic in puffing those flat rounds into giant, soft oyster crackers. These are the simplest of all naturally leavened breads to make. If your oven is hot, and you bake on a hot hearth, low in the oven, pitas virtually never fail to puff. I prefer to bake these on a hearthstone or on tiles, but have also been successful using a preheated baking sheet.

The dough I use for these is, again, the same that I use for making my daily fare—often I will decide to make pita when unexpected events change the schedule of my day and it becomes obvious that I can't wait around for another two hours for the loaves to proof. In half an hour a batch of bread becomes a stack of pockets. If puffing is the measure of success for these, it seems to make no difference whether you shape and bake two hours after mixing or six, although four to six hours gives marginally better flavor.

Divide your dough into oversize golf-ball pieces and round each one. Place the balls on a floured surface and cover well to protect from drying and crusting. Preheat the oven to 500°F. You will need a peel for this, but you don't have to have anything special. I've been using the same flap from a corrugated box for the last ten or twelve months. Dust the peel with flour.

Using a rolling pin, flatten as many balls into rounds as will fit on your baking surface. They should be something less than a quarter-inch thick. Too thick and they won't puff. If you handle the pin too roughly or roll the breads too thin, they will puff only in places. Place the unbaked rounds on the flour-dusted peel. Deftly slide them onto the preheated hearthstone or baking sheet, close the oven, re-dust the peel, and roll out another set.

Three minutes is about all the breads in the oven need. They should puff up like blowfish, brown lightly on the bottom, and not get hard on top. Keep the eye in the back of your head on them as you roll. I've got my timing down so that I finish rolling the last in a set just as the previous set is done baking. I can't think of a reason to go any faster. Brush the hearth with a dry cloth between sets or your later pockets will have burned flour on their surface.

Sesame pita? Just roll the small ball in a bowl of sesame seeds before rolling.

While pita are delicious still warm from the oven, they'll lose any doughiness if allowed to cool completely. They're wonderful for sandwiches of any sort or as single serving loaves of bread to accompany soup and salad. Loaf bread is less than ideal as a travel food due to crumbs and the necessity of slicing. Pita? Crumbless, and no slicing required.

Baking with Rye

RYE WILL THRIVE WHERE WHEAT WILL NOT EVEN SURVIVE. IT WILL PRODUCE A CROP ON THIN, SANDY SOILS OF LOW FERTILITY. IT WILL germinate and grow at temperatures barely above freezing. Rye, when planted in the fall, will survive in its dormant phase extended periods of sub-zero temperatures. As the snow melts and the ground thaws, rye will begin its growth anew at temperatures that keep the wheat asleep.

These qualities were not lost on the farmers of northern and eastern Europe who faced a marginal climate and varying soils. The classic rye breads come from these same areas: Germany, Lithuania, Russia, Scandinavia. Each area developed its own breads, making the best use of local resources to nourish their hearty peasants.

Whether you live in Minnesota or in Georgia, you can enjoy the hearty goodness of naturally leavened rye breads. To most U.S. bread eaters rye bread tastes of caraway and has a dark brown color. Until recently it was difficult, virtually impossible, to find a loaf of rye bread without caraway and without caramel coloring. Even many natural foods bakers color their rye bread with dark molasses or grain coffee. Rye bread is not dark brown or black. Rye does not taste of caraway. Whole-grain rye flour has a grayish cast and a deep "earthy" scent. Bread made from it is dark, but certainly not the chocolate hue common to artificially (or naturally) colored rye bread. Its flavor is not the spiciness of caraway, but is full and satisfying. None of the breads that follow are colored. Only two have seeds and they are optional in one of those. These are the essential rye breads.

Like the varieties of bread in the previous chapter the recipes that follow are all based on the basic method, with the exception of Vollkornbrot and even that is a variation on the theme.

Rye is not wheat. Its flour cannot be substituted for wheat flour without making changes in water, proofing and baking temperatures, dough consistency, mixing and kneading procedures, and proofing and baking times. Nor without changes in your expectations. Rye bread, even with only one cup of rye flour in two loaves, is moister, denser, and earthier tasting than bread made exclusively with wheat.

A dough made with rye flour will ferment more quickly than one made with wheat flour. Use cooler water when mixing and keep the dough below 80°F at least until the final proofing. The little gluten in rye flour is different than that in wheat and is more fragile. Handle with care, kneading and shaping gently to avoid tearing the dough. If the dough seems on the edge of tearing, I will use water-moistened hands and board rather than flour-dusted for shaping loaves.

A rye dough can be very sticky if you let it get that way. Don't. I have found that getting all the flour and all the water well mixed quickly prevents this messy problem. Keep your hands and the kneading surface moistened as you work the dough. You will find that rye bread does better with less kneading than does wheat bread. If one out of the five cups of flour is rye, I might stop kneading at 500 strokes instead of 600 if the dough begins to get a little sticky. With 2 cups, I don't give it a chance to get sticky, but usually stop kneading after 500 strokes, regardless. If all five and a half cups are rye, 300 strokes is enough. If a dough with a good measure of rye flour begins to turn sticky or even slimy while kneading, *stop kneading.* Smooth the dough, return it to the bowl, and cover.

This sticky quality of rye is attributed to gums known as penotosans. These gums are less of a problem in an acid dough than in an alkaline dough. A straight, non-sour dough made with rye flour will be alkaline. Acid "conditions" the dough, making it less sticky, easier to work, and less likely to tear. Hence, the popularity of sourdough rye bread. The acid in the starter, and those that are produced as the microorganisms continue to work, condition the dough. However, many sourdough rye breads rely on the starter only for flavor and conditioning, but use baker's yeast for rising the loaf. Other sour rye breads just have acids introduced into the dough and use no starter or leaven at all.

Not so the breads herein. All are leavened only with leavening, that same community of creatures that you have been using to make the assorted whole wheat breads in the previous chapters.

Just as I don't consider it realistic to have an entirely different recipe for each different variety of bread, nor do I find it worth the trouble to keep a separate starter going just for rye breads. For virtually all of the rye bread that I make, even Rye with a Capital R and Vollkornbrot, I use my usual wheat starter to make the leaven. A wheat-based starter will leaven rye bread as well as, perhaps better than, a rye-based starter. Unless you want rye-only bread for medicinal or esthetic reasons, one starter culture is enough to maintain. At times, it will seem like more than enough.

If, after all this, you still want to use a special rye starter for your rye bread, try the following method, which uses your wheat starter as a base.

Divide the starter ball in half. Add ½ cup water and one cup whole wheat flour to one half. Knead until smooth, and re-wrap. Dissolve the other half in 1¼ cup water. Add 2½ cups freshly milled rye flour, mix, and knead until smooth. Allow to ripen for at least 14 hours, longer if you want a distinct sour flavor, but remember that if you let it go too long it will lose some of its leavening power. If you want to maintain a separate rye leaven make a starter ball from this mature rye leaven.

BARELY RYE BREAD

2 cups leaven
2 cups water
1-2 teaspoons salt
1 cup whole rye flour
4½ cups whole wheat flour

No, the barley hasn't been left out of the recipe. It's just that it has *barely* enough rye flour to call it rye bread. But it has enough so that it's distinctly not a wheat-only bread. You can mix, knead, proof, and bake this as you would the all-wheat bread in the previous chapter, but the rye will impart special flavor, the crumb will be moist and darker, and the bread will have a slightly better keeping quality than all-wheat bread. Some bakers will call this "pain d'campagne," but I prefer to call it what it is. Name yours after Great-Aunt Hilda or what you will, but enjoy it with hearty soup, open-faced sandwiches, or just on its own.

DEFINITELY RYE

2 cups leaven
2⅛ cups water
1-2 teaspoons salt

2 cups rye flour
3½ cups whole wheat flour

It may not be the definitive rye bread, but there's no question that there's some rye in it. Full-flavored, dark, chewy, moist, and ever so slightly sour. With nearly half the non-leaven flour being rye, this bread will benefit from the conditioning effects of an extra-sour leaven. Make the leaven a full 24 hours before you plan to mix the dough. At about 16 hours, set aside 2 cups, refresh the rest as you normally would. You could try to push the leaven beyond 24 hours, but you'll sacrifice leavening power for sourness, and at some point the bread will be unpleasantly sour and heavy.

Dissolve the leaven in 1¾ cups water, add the salt, and stir to dissolve. Blend the rye and whole wheat flours in a bowl. Add the leaven-water-salt to the flours, mix thoroughly with moistened hands, adding the rest of the water, as needed. Work briskly but not roughly. As the dough comes together, turn it out onto your moistened kneading surface and continue kneading for 250 strokes. Cover the dough and let rest for 5 minutes, then knead for another 250 strokes. Keep your hands and the surface moistened to prevent the dough from sticking, but not so wet that the dough slides around. Return to bowl, cover and let sit at cool room temperature for 2 to 3 hours. With moistened hands, give the dough a few turns in the bowl. An hour later, divide the dough in half, shape the loaves, proof and bake as in the standard recipe. Because this bread can be a little more dense than an all-wheat loaf, you may want to decrease the baking temperature by 25°F and increase the baking time slightly.

LEAVENED LIMPE

To either of the above recipes add the grated rind (just the outermost layer) of two organically grown oranges and a teaspoon each of anise and caraway seeds. This bread has a lovely fragrance with a delicate, understated sweetness.

RYE WITH A CAPITAL R

2 cups leaven (rye or wheat)
2½ cups water
1-2 teaspoons salt
5½ cups whole rye flour

This is my version of a rye bread I had first at Ponce's French Bakery in Chico, California, and of a very similar one that I had later from Poilane's in Paris. It is just whole rye flour, salt, water, and leaven. These simple, hearth-baked loaves are delicious, beautiful, essential food. And when everything goes just right (and it usually does) as close to perfect as a bread can be.

I shied away from all-rye bread for years. Then a few years ago I had no choice. We had rye of our own growing, but had to buy the wheat for our baking. It wasn't that we couldn't buy wheat. We could, and did, and used it in most of our baking. But our own bread, we felt, should require only our own grain. The salt, alas, we bought. The bread was baked in an oven built with our own hands and fired with hand-split wood. Ah, yes, this was bread. And it still is, even when made with someone else's rye and baked in the Hotpoint. I urge you to try it now. There is no need to wait for your bread patch of tall waving rye to ripen. And it bakes nearly as well in a baking bell as it does in a wood-fired masonry oven.

Dissolve the leaven in 2 cups water, add the salt and dissolve. Add all the flour, without mixing. With wet hands mix everything together, first by squeezing the mixture, then with a kneading motion as the dough begins to come together. Add the remaining water as you mix. Keep your hands moist and work quickly, but do not handle the dough roughly. I've made this bread for several years and I still expect the dough to be a sticky mess. I'm always surprised at how easy it is to work and how clean my hands are when I'm through. Knead the dough for 300 strokes. Return to bowl, cover, and leave for 2 hours at cool room temperature. With moist hands remove dough to moistened work surface and knead a few strokes. Divide the dough into two loaves, round and put in two well flour-dusted, cloth-lined baskets, or oiled, covered casseroles. Proof, covered, at 80° to 85°F for 1½ hours. Preheat oven to 400°F. The dough should be just beginning to show "stretch marks" and have increased in volume by one-third to one-half.

Often the top crust of this type of bread is not cut, but allowed to break where it will in the oven. I will sometimes make a diagonal cross-hatch pattern, cutting not more than ¼-inch deep. The contrasting dark brown of the cuts and the nearly white of the dusting flour makes for an attractive loaf.

Bake for 45 minutes in a stoneware bell, leaving covered the entire time. If you bake in a covered casserole, remove the cover after 40 minutes and allow to brown for 5 to 15 minutes. The crust should be chewy, but not thick and knife-breaking hard. The crumb should be fine textured and moist and not at all doughy.

VOLLKORNBROT

Whole-corn bread. Corn meaning grain, and in this classic bread from Germany the grain is rye. A dense, all-rye bread, full of pre-cooked whole grains.

1½ (generous) cups whole-grain rye berries
2 cups leaven
2 teaspoons salt
3 cups water
8 cups rye flour
(a tablespoon each of ground caraway and coriander seed is optional)

Make your leaven in the morning the day before you intend to bake this bread. That evening, bring 3 cups of water to a boil, wash and drain rye berries, and add to boiling water. Remove from flame, cover, and let sit overnight.

The following morning drain the berries, reserving the liquid to use as part of the 3 cups water in the recipe. Dissolve leaven and salt in 3 cups water, add the drained berries. If you are including the ground seeds, blend them with the flour now. Add and mix in the flour as in the previous recipe. Add more water if necessary. Knead just until the dough is smooth, perhaps only 150 strokes. Let rise, covered, until quite spongy, perhaps 3 hours.

Divide into two loaves. Oil two standard bread pans. Shape the loaves and gently press into the pans. Proof as above until top surface begins to show fissures. Set oven to 425°F (do not preheat!). Cover pans with foil and place on lower rack. One hour later reduce temperature to 225°F and bake for 3 hours. Remove foil, increase temperature to 350°F and bake for one more hour.

There are many traditional German versions of Vollkornbrot, and some require immersing the bread pans in a larger pan of water and leaving the whole shebang in the oven for 24 hours. The secret is long, slow cooking. The flavor is rich and sweet, almost like caramel. Let the loaves sit for at least a day before serving. If the crust is very hard, wrap in a moist dish towel and refrigerate for a day. Slice very thin. Serve with cream cheese or a fine-textured mild cheese, cider, good lager, or a German wine with just the right fruitiness.

Pizza, European Style

I HAVE THREE DISTINCT MEMORIES OF PIZZA. MY FIRST PIZZA WAS AS A SMALL TOWN TEENAGER ON THE LOOSE IN THE BIG CITY—SPOKANE, Washington—late one night. The little place on a side street, like everything else in town except the police station and the emergency room, was closed for the night, but mama and papa were busy painting the walls. One of my buddies was bold enough to walk in and ask them if they'd make us a pizza anyway. Amid much to-do, our gang of six was ushered to a high-back booth, papa retired to the kitchen, and mama kept us in conversation and laughter until the pizza arrived. Ah, this was food! Thick, spongy crust, spicy sauce, and stretchy cheese. My Puritan New England mother hadn't prepared me for such sensuous eating.

My next memorable pizza didn't arrive for almost twenty years, and it wasn't really a pizza, but the French version, *pissaladiere*. My wife and I were driving through Provence on a sunny Sunday morning in May and we stopped for lunch in the market square of a small village. A corner bakery offered pissaladiere, topped with tomatoes and olives and latticed with anchovies. The crust was identical (to my memory after twenty years) to that first late-night pizza in Spokane, the tomato topping richly flavored with Provencal olive oil and herbs. Though I'm sure the village fountain, the ancient stone of the buildings on the square, and the Mediterranean beyond the hills all contributed, we both agreed that this was the best pizza, even if it wasn't Italian, that either of us had tasted.

I had to wait only three days for my next memorable pizza experience. This time it was not so much the pizza as the *pizzerie*. Aosta is in the north of Italy, in the Alps just before the road tunnels through to Switzerland. The sunny market square of Provence was only a fond memory, with the mountains blanketed in snow all around and the wind sweeping the darkening streets. Through the corner window of a building in the old section of town we could see the orange flickers of dancing flames. Inside on the left were four or five vinyl upholstered booths with Formica tabletops. On the right was a chest-high counter, and behind that, a brick oven. Through its open-arched door, a fire of seasoned hardwoods from the mountains could be seen. The fire was banked against one side of the domed oven and two pizzas were baking directly on the hearth on the opposite side. Occasionally a gust of wind would blow the scent of woodsmoke into the room. The cook was shaping risen balls of dough into discs, placing them on a wooden peel, quickly dressing them with sauce, slices of local cheese, and various toppings, and finishing them off with a dash of herbs before sliding them into the oven. Once the crust was set, he deftly rotated the pizza to keep the side nearest the fire from charring before the rest of the pizza could cook. Our pizza was perfectly baked, the dough now crusty and chewy, with just a hint of oaksmoke from the fire.

In the time since our joint trip to Europe, we've eaten and made many pizzas—less memorable, perhaps, but delicious, varied, and nourishing. Basically, pizza is simple food. In its simplest form, it's bread hot from the oven, topped with a brushing of olive oil and a dash of fresh herbs. As it gets more complicated, it is often topped with vegetables, tomatoes, cheese, and seafood, and becomes nearly a meal in itself. Once you understand that pizza is just a thin round of bread baked with something on top, the concept can be extended to any type of cuisine and the topping adapted to season and locale. Such is the origin of pizza in Italian cuisine. Pizza was food for the peasant farming and fishing people of the Italian countryside. Its base, the staff of life; the toppings, the fruits of the gardens, fields, mountains, and sea. Pizza then is a peasant landscape, painted by generations of farmers, fisherfolk, and cooks.

Making a good sourdough pizza crust is much simpler than making a good, high-rising loaf of naturally leavened bread—with pizza you *want* flat bread!

SOURDOUGH CRUST

Several years ago I was cooking for myself and working all day on a local organic produce farm. Before I left the house in the morning I would make a simple dough of freshly milled whole wheat flour, water, and a pinch of starter. After kneading, I'd put the dough in a bowl, cover it with a damp cloth and a plate, and put it to rise in a warm spot. When I came home from work I'd pinch off a small ball of dough for the next day's starter and shape the remaining dough into a round. I'd let the pizza rise while I washed off the day's dirt, then brush it with oil, top it with fresh basil and oregano and perhaps a bit of garlic, and pop it in the oven. In half an hour, I was feasting on the best of breads and generous portions of vegetables from the farm. The leftover bread found its way into my lunchbox for the next day.

> *¼ cup leaven or sourdough starter*
> *1 cup cool water*
> *whole wheat bread flour*
> *sea salt*

At breakfast time dissolve the starter in one cup cool water. Add a mere pinch of salt and enough flour to make a soft dough. Knead until smooth and elastic. Let the dough rest for 5 minutes, then knead again for 4 minutes. Place the dough in a bowl, cover with damp toweling and a plate, and leave at room temperature. By mid-afternoon the dough should have begun to rise and soften. At about 4:30, deflate the dough and re-cover, perhaps moving it to a slightly warmer spot. An hour before you plan to eat, deflate the dough again and pinch off a piece of dough for your starter. Shape the remaining dough into a ball and let rest, covered, for 5 minutes.

Roll (or toss) into a round and place on an oiled tin or stoneware base sprinkled with cornmeal or coarse flour. Cover and let rise in a warm spot for 25 minutes. The dough is now ready for any of the recipes that follow.

All of the pizzas that follow should be baked in a hot oven, 500° to 575°F. These recipes will make an 8-inch-diameter, thick "bread" crust or an 11- or 12-inch, thin-crusted pizza. We usually use a thick crust for a simple oil and herb pizza and a thin for the fancier ones, but the choice is yours. When rolling out a thin pizza, make the round an inch bigger than you want the pizza to be and fold this extra dough in on itself to make a bready edge-crust.

An otherwise perfect pizza is ruined by a doughy crust. This is the result of an under-risen dough, oven temperature either too high or too low, too thick of a dough, or too much topping on the pizza. A shiny pizza pan will make it nearly impossible to get a well-baked whole wheat crust. Because the top of the crust is covered with your selected fillings, the bread relies on bottom heat for most of its cooking. A shiny stainless steel pan reflects heat instead of absorbing it.

Cast iron, black bakers' steel, or stoneware all make better pizzas.

OIL AND HERB PIZZA

Delicious food couldn't be easier: Just brush a risen thick round with olive oil and top with crushed basil and oregano. The herbs could be replaced or complemented with crushed garlic for an *aglio e olio* pizza. Bake in a hot oven until nicely browned, about 25 minutes. Simpler yet is *Pizza alla Romana*, topped just with oil and a sprinkling of sea salt.

PIZZA BIANCA

Literally white pizza, the onion lover's delight with mountains of slender crescents cooked down into a buttery topping.

4 medium onions
olive oil
water
rosemary or thyme

Peel the onions and slice into thin crescents. Heat 2 teaspoons olive oil in a skillet. Sauté the onions on a high flame, stirring constantly for a minute or two until they turn translucent—don't let them scorch! Reduce the heat to medium-low and cover. Stir occasionally. The onions are done when soft and buttery, maybe 20 minutes or half an hour. Spread the onions evenly on a risen crust. Top with a few raw thin-sliced onion rings, and lightly brush with olive oil. Sprinkle with crushed fresh rosemary or thyme and bake. For added zest, finish it with a touch of freshly ground black peppercorns just as it comes from the oven. Attractively arranged walnut halves added before baking (delete the raw onions and black pepper) add an elegant touch to this simple pizza.

PIZZA AL PESTO

Another of the simple, traditional pizzas of Italy—just a round of bread dough, half baked, then spread with pesto and baked until done. This pesto recipe makes enough for several pizzas. Use the extra on pasta, as a spread on whole wheat bread, in salad dressings, or on another pizza.

3 cups (packed) fresh basil leaves, washed and well dried
¾ cup olive oil

½ cup pine nuts
½ - 1 teaspoon sea salt
3 cloves garlic

Chop the basil very finely, combine with the remaining ingredients, and pound and grind with a mortar and pestle until everything is ground and bound together. To make the pizza, brush a risen round with oil, bake for 15 minutes, remove from the oven, spread with pesto, garnish with fresh basil leaves, and return to the oven for 10 or 15 minutes.

PIZZA NAPOLETANA

This is the basic tomato and cheese pizza that was the source of what we have come to know as pizza in this country. Many recipes call for a topping of long-simmered Neapolitan sauce, rich with garlic and herbs. Much simpler is to use chopped tomatoes, oil, garlic, and herbs and let the sauce make itself as the pizza bakes. Of course, this is best with paste-type tomatoes, fresh from the garden, but canned will work well in the off-season. Extra-thin slices of cheese mean less cheese overall and less fat than usual for this familiar type of pizza.

5 tomatoes, peeled
2 ounces mozzarella cheese, sliced very thinly
oregano or basil
sea salt
garlic, crushed
olive oil

Chop the tomatoes and spread on a risen pizza round. Arrange the cheese slices, and sprinkle with the herbs and a touch of salt. Add crushed garlic, and pour a teaspoon or two of olive oil on top. Bake at a slightly lower temperature than other recipes to keep the cheese from burning before the crust is baked. Optional toppings include all the usual stuff: anchovies, bell pepper (oven-roasted first), ripe olives, blanched broccoli or cauliflower florets. Thin slices of fried tofu or tempeh go well on top, though they aren't very traditional in Italy.

PISSALADIERE

This is the pizza of Provence, once sold at every corner, fresh from the oven, in the Latin quarters of Marseille and Toulon. It is now also known as *Pizza Provencal* and is available far from the Mediterranean in the food markets on the streets of Paris.

olive oil
3 onions, cut as for Pizza Bianca
sea salt
2 or 3 peeled, chopped tomatoes
15 pitted ripe olives
2 ounces anchovies, well drained and soaked in cold water
for 15 minutes to remove excess salt

Sauté the onions in the oil as for Pizza Bianca, adding a pinch of salt and the tomatoes just before they're done. Spread the onion mixture on the risen dough—which is invariably rectangular—and arrange the anchovies in a diagonal latticed pattern. Place an olive in the center of each resulting diamond. Bake.

PIZZA AUX FRUITS DE MER

Another of the pizzas of southeastern France, also known as Provencal seafood pizza, this is hearty, delicious, and beautiful.

½ pound shrimp
½ pound cleaned squid, cut into ¼-inch-thick rings
½ pound mussels
olive oil
sea salt
3 or 4 peeled, chopped tomatoes
2 cloves garlic
15-20 pitted, oil-cured olives
a few sprigs fresh thyme

Boil the shrimp in salted water until they float, drain immediately, peel and devein. Sauté the squid for 3 minutes over a medium flame. Steam the mussels until the shells open, then drain. Spread chopped tomatoes on the risen dough, and sprinkle a pinch of salt and the crushed garlic on top. Arrange the cooked seafood and top with crushed thyme and 2 teaspoons olive oil. Strategically place olives and bake.

OTHER POSSIBILITIES

Blanched spinach, broccoli, roasted eggplant rounds, artichokes, mushrooms—not just the common varieties but all sorts of wild and exotic species including shiitake, tree ear, oyster, boletus, shaggy mane—all make for fine pizza, as do virtually any precooked seafood and fish, and the fruits of your garden. One evening, with nothing in the larder except a few leeks and some cold baked potatoes and already risen dough we made what must have been a pizza, bread topped with sweet sautéed leeks and slices of the peeled, cooked potatoes. When it was baked, the potatoes were browned on top and the juices from the leeks had penetrated the crust. Certainly not Italian—perhaps Irish, or Welsh?—but delicious.

Building the
Backyard Bake Oven

A S I COAST DOWN THE SLOPE ON LAWRENCE
STREET IN PORT TOWNSEND, WASHINGTON,
THE AROMA OF FRESH-BAKED BREAD GRABS
me by the nose and pulls me around the corner onto Adams street
and into the driveway at the Lunde house. Gunda Lunde has just
opened the stucco-faced brick oven in the little courtyard between the
garage and the guest cottage, and is removing the dozen crusty, round
loaves of sour rye from the brick hearth with a long-handled wooden
peel. Little more than a half hour ago, she deftly placed the risen
loaves directly on the hot brick hearth using this same paddle-shaped,
flat wooden shovel, a magical feat much like the old tablecloth-and-
dishes trick. An hour before that, the three-foot-long, oval baking
chamber was a swirling inferno of blazing maple and alder.

With the breads on their wooden cooling rack, Gunda places a
clay pot full of rice on the peel, deposits it to the back corner of the
oven, then slides in a neighbor's plumcake dessert. When these are
done she'll put in a beanpot for overnight simmering.

It's hard to resist sampling the shiny, deep-reddish brown, high-
rising loaves, still crackling from the oven's heat. Earlier bakes of
Gunda's bread from her new oven have been superb—her best bread
since moving here from her native Germany several years ago. And
this batch, she says, looks even better. But we do resist , knowing the
loaves need to cool before being broken. The resistance, however, is
not an act of patience and extreme discipline. While the fire was still
burning in the oven, Gunda made a dozen pita breads, one of which

she offers me once she has sealed the oven door to bake the rice and plumcake.

This oven is not something built from esoteric Old German plans handed down through the centuries. Bjorn Lunde, a Norwegian-American and Gunda's husband, and I built the oven with the help of Alan Scott, a northern California oven designer and home-baker extraordinaire. The masonry oven and its concrete cladding (coating) were completed in less than the four days of Scott's short Port Townsend visit, and the oven housing and insulation required only one more day's work. We used only materials available either in Bjorn's salvage pile or from local building suppliers. One of the principal builders—me—had never laid a brick in his life. Now there I was, not just laying flat courses, but setting bricks in the graceful arch forming the oven's vaulted chamber.

The oven was simple to build from Scott's plans, taking only a few days from start to finish, and cost less than a new gas range. The oven imparts a quality to bread and other foods like nothing you've had from your gas or electric kitchen range. Its breads are remarkably high-rising, wonderfully crusty, and indescribably delicious. Pizza in the brick oven becomes a new food, and salmon from the local waters—you'd have to taste it to know.

I don't get much of a kick out of watching the oven in my kitchen range heat up, but I'm mesmerized by the flames swirling and dancing across the vaulted ceiling of this oven. I could sit for hours watching the flame; indeed, only the need to tend the rising bread keeps me from doing so. There is magic in the sweeping of the oven, with hissing steam rising from the wet broom; magic in the smell of the cornmeal-dusted loaves as they settle onto the hot hearth, and in the miracle of the loaves and fishes that emerge from the mouth of the oven, transformed to new life by the fire stored in the bricks.

If you plan to build a brick oven, be forewarned: this is not a microwave, modern convenience oven—pop in your frozen entree, push a button, and be dining in twenty-three seconds flat. Your wood-fired brick oven will invite you to plan your days and focus on fire and food. Its warmth and fire will bring you, your family, and friends together around its cheery mouth for many meals. The bread that emerges will be the best you have ever tasted, and will nourish in more ways than we can ever know.

RETAINED-HEAT BREAD OVENS

Retained-heat ovens are at least as old as baking, have been successfully built of adobe, clay, stone, brick, and concrete, and are used daily in most parts of the world today. Their continued popularity, although threatened by the present global firewood crisis, is bound to increase if for no other reason than that forests and other biomass crops may have to supplant modern nonrenewable and hazardous energy sources in the near future.

To build a retained-heat oven today we have the advantages of a wide range of suitable materials and techniques and a vast reservoir of knowledge from many sources. They promise some exciting new-and-improved oven designs that are simpler in construction, with increased performances and fuel efficiencies, and with some brand new virtues, like portability.

The oven whose plans we present here preserves a direct link with traditional handicrafts and our culinary roots and processes. But it is only one approach. We hope that our explanation of the principles of brick oven building will allow you to be creative in your oven design and construction.

All retained-heat ovens operate by the same principle: A fire is kept burning in a baking chamber long enough so that the chamber, after the fire is removed, will hold enough heat to bake bread on the same hearth that supported the fire.

Primarily responsible for producing loaves of unbelievable splendor is the three-way heat of these ovens. It radiates off the walls, penetrating everything inside like microwaves; it conducts off the hearth directly into the unpanned loaves that sit on the bricks; and it circulates around the loaves carried by the steam escaping from the baking dough. This all-pervasive heat bakes the largest loaves (four-pound whole-grain loaves, for example) in about half the time of that of a gas or electric oven. Brick ovens guarantee the maximum "spring" in a loaf, because the steamy environment in a tightly sealed oven keeps the crust pliable and the loaf expanding well into the bake. The fragrant steam emanating from the fermented dough gradually bakes itself onto the crust and gives the bread a unique flavor. That same all-important steam also accounts for the characteristic sheen on the rich brown crusts of brick-oven baked breads.

DESIGN REQUIREMENTS

A bread oven's ceiling should be low enough to concentrate the steam, but not so low that the crust scorches; fifteen inches is satisfactory. Above eighteen inches, steam dissipates and the heat becomes less effective. Vents, flues, dampers, ash dumps, and large doors not only reduce heat-retaining mass, but also leak valuable steam and let in unwanted cold drafts. You won't find them in a good oven, which must both draw air for the fire and expel smoke and fumes through its one small opening—the bread- and wood-loading door at the front.

To heat well, a bread oven must be a long, low rectangular or oblong furnace with a rounded ceiling and sides that funnel gently to the door opening. There should be no nooks, ledges, or corners to collect ash and charcoal, and no areas inaccessible to the ash scraper and wet mop. The flow of air into the oven across the hearth, with the flames rising and curling across the ceiling and the fumes and smoke drawn back out the door and up the flue, should keep the fire burning well but not so well that all the heat goes out with the smoke. The door height should be little less than two-thirds that of the height of the dome.

A retained-heat oven must have just enough mass in its hearth, wall, and dome material to store the heat necessary for baking, with the hearth more massive than the rest by about 33 percent. The denser the material the better. With modern materials and technology, design can be refined to suit a particular need; and with comprehensive insulation, such an oven can be impressively efficient.

An oven with a quick fire-up time, with heat for only a single batch of bread (but with several hours of gradually diminishing baking heat) can be constructed from a single layer of bricks laid on edge, that is, four inches thick, with the hearth also of bricks on edge laid over a two-inch slab of concrete. On the same hearth, an oven cast in two-inch-thick concrete will perform similarly. An oven built on a solid base, with foot-thick sand- or rubble-filled top and sides, will bake several batches of bread from the one fairly long firing. The middle way is the most popular: a two-to-three-inch-thick concrete hearth slab topped by hearth bricks on edge, with a three-inch-thick cast concrete oven or one constructed with a layer of bricks on edge beefed up by one-to-two inches of concrete over all. This last oven design, of a size large enough for a dozen loaves at a batch and other uses that best suit a family, is the one we have chosen to describe in detail.

BEFORE YOU BEGIN

A few pre-manufactured wood-fired retained-heat ovens are on the market mainly for commercial use. They are expensive, but prices should drop as popularity rises. Less expensive units come as kits, but they require some effort to assemble. The number of masons with experience in oven design or construction is growing, but the best option is still building your own oven. With basic skills and equipment and inexpensive materials, you can have in a week or two an oven that is almost indestructible, that requires virtually no maintenance, that is efficient by any standard, that can use home-grown renewable fuel, and bakes bread that is without compare.

This oven needs to be fully loaded to create the steam that bakes the best bread, so construct a size that will bake your usual needs in one batch. The remaining hours of heat can then be used for more bread (there should be plenty of heat for a second batch) and the traditional possibilities that best use the gradually diminishing heat of the oven: pies, cakes, cookies, crackers, casseroles, sprouted-wheat "Essene" breads, puddings, fruits and vegetables, jams and custards, dried foods and herbs, yogurt, and eventually drying the kindling and wood for the next firing. A well-insulated oven will take days to cool down.

Decide next if you are willing to compromise the oven design, making the chamber and door a little wider for pizzas, pita, and matzoh crackers that need a continuously burning fire during the bake. Decide also on the materials for the oven base and case, so that you can finalize plans and gather materials.

Choosing a site is important. The whole structure requires an area roughly four by five feet to stand on, plus room for a solid footing. It will rise to a height of five feet not counting the flue, which needs at least two or three more feet but can extend to almost any height if necessary. There will be some smoke at the beginning of a firing, which may determine the location of your oven.

The oven should be placed within practical range of the kitchen or the kneading, shaping, and proofing area, particularly the latter. If you are considering an indoor location, be prepared for major remodeling, a lengthy planning and permit process, and added expenses for flue, ash disposal and cleanout, detailing, finish work, and so on.

Protecting the oven opening from wind is important to its draft and heating performance. If you are going to use your oven year round, you will need a roof, at least over the baker and the bread dough poised at the top of its proof as it is loaded. You need plenty of elbow room to set, stir, rake out, and mop the oven, and for handling proofed loaves and peeling them into and out of the oven onto cooling racks. You may want a dry storage area for wood, with perhaps space to expand the operations later to include room for milling, a grainery, proof cabinet, cooling racks, and other conveniences.

For private use outdoors a small bread oven will legally pass as a barbecue. Indoors it must be treated as a fireplace at least. For commercial use, except on a farm in some special cases, the health regulations must be met, and even for home compliance you should consult with planning, fire, and health authorities together so that misunderstandings and duplications can be avoided.

A STEP-BY-STEP GUIDE

Footing

Mark out the trench for the footing and dig it down to firm sub-soil stratum below the frost line. Fill the trench with coarse gravel and top the gravel with a layer of concrete. Add reinforcing to the concrete if you feel it is necessary.

Base

This reinforced base is designed to be lifted, the oven with it, by suitable fork-lift equipment and moved, if necessary.

The concrete base will be topped with a layer of hearth bricks laid on edge 4-inches thick, so before you construct the form you should determine the most comfortable hearth height and size the base accordingly.

Using new or recycled plywood at least ½-inch thick, construct the forms to pour the base legs and oven hearth to the dimensions shown in the plans and to your custom height. Brace the forms well to avoid bulging, and stake them firmly in place on the square and level.

For extra heat efficiency you can insulate under the base with non-flammable rigid insulation board or panels. Allow extra depth in the form to accommodate the insulation, and place it in the form before the concrete is poured. So that it will adhere to the base, poke flat-head nails through it first so that the points will end up imbedded in the concrete.

Bend the reinforcing bar and wire it in place before you pour the concrete. Tamp the concrete down into the form with a short length of rebar as you pour to ensure that the form is completely filled, and tap the sides with a hammer to further settle it. Screeding off the slab top is the only finish needed except perhaps for running an edging tool around the perimeter.

There is little need for elaborate wet or long curing of the base; its strength is adequate without it. As soon as the concrete is set the hearth bricks can be laid.

Hearth Bricks

Use hard, dense firebricks—even the cheaper ones made like house bricks work well—but do not use the lightweight heat reflective firebricks that are popular today for potter's kilns.

Mix a mortar of sand and fireclay 50/50 and butter it onto the base ½-inch deep or less, enough to lay two rows of bricks. This weak mortar allows you to set the hearth bricks precisely, so there are no protrusions that could trip the peel as the oven is loaded. Also, broken or worn bricks can easily be replaced in the future. Use a wooden mallet to tap them into place; use no mortar between the bricks but keep them as tight up together as possible. (Mortar between the bricks would wear off onto the bread.)

Let the final row of hearth bricks protrude over the base to form a lip. Mortar underneath and between for extra strength.

Try to keep sand, dust, and other debris from the cracks between the bricks so there is no expansion and shifting later. The wood ash will fill them.

Oven Bricks

Red bricks are adequate, but choose them for their density. A good dense brick is usually heavy and hard and a little more costly. Do not use soft or hollow bricks, or lightweight firebricks.

There are two nationally available common red bricks. The oven plans here are drawn using the larger "standard" brick which in the California area measures exactly 3 inches thick, 2½ inches high, and 8¼ inches long. If you use the popular "modular" bricks, 10 percent smaller in height and length than the "standard" brick, your oven will turn out correspondingly smaller so you will need to make adjustments.

Unlike regular brickwork, the bricks of this oven are held together with less mortar, only about ¼-inch. The mortar mix is modified by using extra fireclay, making a mortar that will harden with heat rather than soften, as is the case with simple cement/sand mortars. Fireclay adds a sticky quality to the mortar that helps to form this novel oven shape. The mortar mix is 10 parts sand, 3 parts cement, and 1½ parts fireclay. Bricks should be briefly dunked in water before buttering and laying them.

Side Walls

1. Without mortar, stand up all the bricks of the first course of the oven, judging the ¼-inch space between them for mortar and making certain all is in place as planned, particularly the two doorjamb bricks. Mark their outline with a thick carpenter's crayon.

2. Remove the bricks and begin to mortar them in place, beginning with the two doorjamb bricks to be sure that they end up exactly opposite each other.

3. Next, mortar in place the bricks that make up the entrance up to the height of the upright bricks, being sure that they are positioned ¾-inch wider at each side than the upright door-jamb bricks.

4. Lay the rest of the bricks. Remember to keep the mortar to a minimum thickness, but not so thin as to make the going slow and

difficult. As the work progresses keep sponging off the excess mortar and keep the bricks clean on the inside faces. A drop cloth over the hearth is essential.

5. Place an angle iron on top of 1-inch-thick slices of brick mortared to the tops of the upright doorjamb bricks to give the opening the exact height of 10 inches. See that the jambs and angle iron lintel end up on the same plane so that the door will seat well.

Keep sponging the excess mortar off all the brickwork as the oven grows. (There is no easy way to reach in afterwards.) A final wash of three parts water to one part vinegar will remove the last traces of cement bloom from the bricks, best done after it dries some.

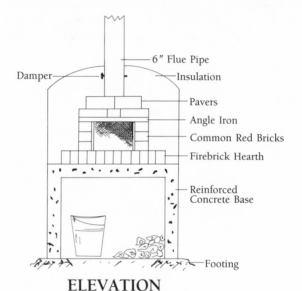

ELEVATION

SECTION

Vaulted Roof

Next comes the exciting part of laying the vaulted arches of the roof, but first there is some preparation.

1. Two templates for laying the arch must be made in plywood. Mark off the inside width of the oven along the bottom straight edge of a sheet. At each end of this line mark a point 8 inches above corresponding to the height of the side walls of the oven. From the midpoint of this line make a point 15 inches above marking the height of the dome. Now lightly sketch in a long, low arch that connects these three points, and then stand on end the necessary number of bricks to form this span, each brick touching its neighbor on the inside of the arch, and tilted to be evenly spaced on the outside. Flatten out the arch as much as you dare in the center, but keep a curve in it, and bring it down as abruptly as possible at the ends where the

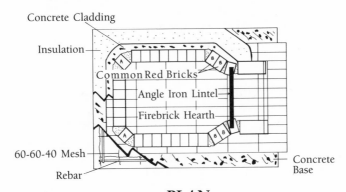

PLAN

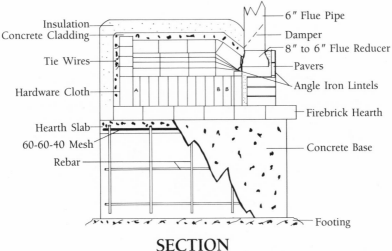

SECTION

arch will meet the walls. With a marker trace the line of the bricks, following faithfully their every facet, and cut out two of these templates with a saber saw.

Nail the templates to the opposite sides of a short length of 2 x 4 and the form is ready to place in position spanning the oven walls on a ¼-inch spacer of cardboard on two upright bricks at the rear of the oven.

2. It helps now to pile up some bricks vertically on top of the rear wall as a guide to laying the arch that must come within ¼-inch of it to allow for mortar later.

3. Since there is some outward thrust exerted by the arch, especially when the mortar is green and you are encouraging stubborn bricks to fit, wait until mortar in the walls is firm before proceeding. Brace the walls when you lay the arch.

4. Now lay the arch, starting from each end and working towards the top, being sure that each brick sits accurately on its facet, that each brick touches its neighbor on the bottom, and that they are evenly tilted. The last brick will fit just right if all goes well.

5. The rear wall can now be laid with mortar to meet this arch, inserting a few tie wires into the joints to tie on some reinforcing mesh later. The arch form can now be carefully moved forward ready to support the next arch course.

6. The final roof course bridges the remaining gap without the use of a form and is laid straight beginning from the center following the straight face of the angle iron. The final triangular cavities remaining at each end must be filled with shaped bricks.

Flue and Door

To prevent any smoke escaping, the outside doorway sill should be as low as, or lower than, that of the inner oven door. For an outdoor site this is not so critical and the outer doorway can be wider and taller to give better access to the oven itself.

Use an angle iron lintel support, or, again making up a form in plywood, construct a low brick arch across the very front of the oven entrance. The arch will have to protrude forward an inch or two to leave space inside for the flue, and it will be made from half bricks or less for the same reason.

To funnel the fumes and smoke up and away from the door and for a smooth transition from brick to flue pipe, the oven can have an 8-inch to 6-inch wood burning stove flue reducer (shown in the plan), or a 12 x 14-inch rectangular air conditioner duct "straight boot" that reduces to a 6-inch round flue, or a 12-inch to 6-inch "taper," cut and flared and inserted into the mortar of the brickwork.

When the final flue bricks are laid in place, the cavity around the reducer can be filled with mortar.

Concrete Cladding

An oven built of a single thickness of brick will work well, but the extra mass and strength gained by a simply applied 2-inch layer of concrete makes all the difference.

1. Tie a layer of mesh, hardware cloth, chicken wire, or tightly woven fencing to the rear wall of the oven by the tie wires imbedded in the masonry earlier for this purpose. This should keep the concrete from ever cracking and falling away. The side walls, being much lower, do not need this treatment.

2. To allow for a little expansion of the oven bricks independent of the concrete layer to come, cover the brick vaults with four to six layers of a heavy-duty household aluminum foil sheeting.

3. Cut out two pieces of 6 x 6-inch, 40-gauge reinforcing mesh large enough to fit carefully over the wrapped oven. Shape them around the oven and stagger a little. Tie the mesh pieces together, and prop them ½-inch out from the oven with brick shards.

4. Place plywood formwork 2 inches out from the oven by simply wedging it against the concrete hearth or otherwise boxing in the oven following its shape until the form meets the bricks that make up the doorway. This formwork need only extend up to the top of the walls. The roof can be simply layered on and troweled.

5. When pouring the concrete, tamp it well down into the narrow form with a length of rebar and strike the outside of the form with a hammer to get it to settle.

6. Bring the concrete up to the flue generously, helping to strengthen and support it.

Curing and Drying the Oven

Before use, the oven should be left to cure for at least two weeks, ideally four, if time and patience allow. Before adding the insulation and boxing in the oven is the best time to dry the oven thoroughly by a series of small fires burned in the oven chamber. Begin with very small fires of kindling, three a day for the first three days, then increase the length of these fires by adding wood to keep them burning for several hours at a time for the rest of the week. These should continue to be relatively small, slow fires. A raging inferno would likely dry the masonry too quickly and promote cracking, either now, or later in the oven's life. A low-watt electric heater with a fan also works well, but don't let it run continuously or the oven may heat up too fast as it begins to dry out.

Oven Housing and Insulation

Ovens traditionally have been protected from the elements, particularly the winds that upset air draft, with shelters that protrude forward to include the baker. In some rare cases they have been insulated with a layer of ashes. In hot climates adobe ovens seem to be purposely placed in the sun for solar assistance.

Today it is a simple matter to box in the entire oven and thoroughly insulate it, yielding previously unattainable efficiency. Masonry, wood, or a combination of both are the main choices today. The oven requirements are for a good 6 inches of insulation all over, and protection from water, and so long as these are met style has great flexibility.

Temperatures on the outside of the oven may reach 500°F. Cracks could develop and allow the passage of fire through the walls, so insulating materials must be fireproof. Rock wool and vermiculites both are suitable.

The simplest insulation of all is shown in the plans. The oven is coated, with the use of forms of plywood or waxed cardboard, with a thick layer of a mix of fine vermiculite or pool base and cement 4:1, and for a waterproof skin this layer can be rendered with a cement sand stucco of 1:1.

Oven Accessories

To operate the oven you will need a length of 1½-2-inch pipe, "a draft door," a wooden oven door, a poker, an ash rake (actually, a broad hoe), a natural bristle broom or a rag mop and mop bucket, a covered metal ash can, and a peel.

The draft door is optional but its proper use gives you control over the fire to influence the rate of combustion. It directs outside air to the base of the fire and channels smoke and fumes up the flue.

A mop can be custom-made to the oven by notching a suitable handle to quarter-inch depth, four inches back from the end and placing an eighteen-inch square or two of toweling squarely over it and wiring it tightly into the notch. Fold the towel forward and tie it again two inches back from the end and trim the cloth off straight. For cleaning the hearth after firing, some prefer a "garage floor" broom, cut down to fit through the door, with the long handle mounted flat across the top of the brush, making it easy to pull the broom horizontally across the hearth.

The peel must be at least slightly wider than your largest loaf, but obviously narrower than the oven door. Mine is long enough to load two loaves simultaneously, allowing me to load the oven in half the time, thus limiting oven cooling during loading. The paddle of the peel is sawed or planed from hardwood, and the handle of a lighter wood finished to an octagon in section for a firm grip. The paddle is fastened tightly to the handle by two wire pins. If you bake often, the paddle of your peel will wear thin or split and need replacement. The handle should last as long as you bake.

The oven door should fit tightly and be made of a good two inches of wood to insulate well. The inner face should have thin sheet metal tacked to it, and a convenient handle is that from masonry suppliers sold as replacement handles for concrete finishing floats. Affix the handle vertically for easiest one-handed use.

You need a long poker to stir the fire, and a broad hoe (the rake) to remove coals and ashes. A metal bucket to receive the hot coals and ash and a mop bucket are essentials.

Temperatures during firing reach well over 1,000° F. For a built-in temperature gauge, ceramics suppliers usually have the equipment ready for installation. Glass insulated AWG #20 gauge ANSI type K thermocouple wire and a 1,500° F K-type pyrometer readout are optimal. If you use a thermocouple probe, it should be inserted into one sidewall during construction, halfway between front and back, and halfway between hearth and ceiling. To protect the probe bury it ¼-inch deep in the mortar.

FIRING YOUR OVEN

Once you have properly cured and insulated your oven, you're ready for your first of many firings and subsequent bakings. First lay a length of 1½-2-inch pipe on the hearth. It should extend from just inside the oven door to a point two inches from the center of the back wall. This gets air to the back of the fire for more uniform burning. Start your fire with tinder and kindling at the front of the oven, then gently push the fire toward the back. Stoke the fire with hardwoods, no larger than 2 inches through. Once the fire is burning strongly, stoke it with an armload more of dry, 2-inch hardwood. When this is burning well, close the flue damper part way and partially close the draft door if you are using one. You want a vigorous fire, but not one that roars so much that the heat all goes up the flue.

As the fire burns, the arched interior surfaces will first blacken with soot as the smoke condenses on the cool masonry. About halfway through the firing, the soot begins to burn off, and the bricks turn back to their natural color. This second transition will commence at the crown of the arch, just in front of the heart of the fire and spread outward until the entire dome is clean. During this time you will probably have to toss in another half-armload of fuel. Some references say that when the bricks have burned clean the oven is hot enough. With both of the small ovens I have used, I've found it necessary to burn another half-armload of hardwood sticks to ensure a good, hot bake. Toss these into the fire and spread the fire a bit to ensure even heating.

When the flames have subsided, spread the hot coals over the hearth and close the chimney damper nearly completely and leave just a thin passage for combustion air to enter the oven at the draft door. Twenty to thirty minutes before your bread is ready to bake, remove the pipes and rake the ash and remaining coals into a metal bucket. Cover and set the bucket out of harm's way. In the oxygen-starved atmosphere the glowing coals will self-extinguish and you'll have a few pounds of good charcoal.

Using your oven mop or broom, clean the oven hearth completely. You'll need to periodically immerse the broom or mop in a bucket of water. This both keeps the tool from igniting and helps pick up fine ash from the hearth. Take care to get bits of charcoal from the juncture of the hearth and the back wall of the oven. Work as quickly as you can and still complete the task with both safety and thoroughness. Seal the oven door and let the oven "soak"—even out—for fifteen to twenty minutes.

Bread baking range is 500° to 700°F at rake out (this is the masonry's temperature, not the oven air's). To gauge the temperature without a probe, either reach into the oven and count the seconds before it becomes too hot to bear or toss some flour onto the hearth and watch how fast it browns and remember the results for next time. When too hot, extra wet-mopping and leaving the door off before loading helps. A cup or two of water tossed in with the bread will temper the heat some.

LOADING THE OVEN

These instructions are for loading the oven with loaves of hearth bread that have been proofed upside down in cloth-lined baskets. All you'll need for pan-proofed breads is the peel.

Have on hand: proofed bread, bowl of cornmeal or coarse flour, sharp serrated knife or single-edged razor blade.

This goes better with two people but can be done alone. Work quickly to preserve oven heat.

1. Lightly dust top surface of peel with cornmeal.

2. Invert two cloth-lined baskets with proofed bread onto the peel, one in front of the other.

3. Carefully remove the baskets and cloth, and quickly slash the tops of the loaves with a sharp blade.

4. Insert the peel into the oven, placing it not quite against the

right wall and back of the oven. With a short push, followed by a sharp pull, deposit the loaves on the hearth. Repeat, except place these two loaves next to the first two. To place two more loaves in the other back corner, slant the peel from the floor of the oven above the second pair of loaves and slide the breads from the peel onto the hearth. Continue until all breads are on the hearth. Insert oven door, making sure that you have a tight fit.

It's easier to load the oven with pan-breads. Alan bakes excellent desem-leavened loaves in terra cotta flowerpot bases. Black bakers' pans and sheets also work well. These are all easier to place and can be rearranged on the hearth to make them fit better. With a hearth loaf, you get only one chance for perfect placement. The combination of better flavor, quicker baking, and continuing in an ancient tradition, and the challenge of mastering a new skill make it worthwhile to bake directly on the hearth.

If I am baking only a half-oven of bread (a good idea when first learning) I will put a tin of water on the bricks before sealing the oven door. This tin has small perforations that allow the water to *slowly* leak onto the hearth bricks and replace the steam that the missing breads would otherwise provide. If your bread isn't as shiny as you like, and the crust is dull brown, perhaps there's just not enough moisture in the oven. After loading the bread, and immediately before sealing the door, mist the baking chamber and breads with a garden sprayer reserved only for this use.

Bread bakes incredibly fast in a hot brick oven. It can be thoroughly baked in as little as twenty-five minutes, though forty is more common. Some loaves, depending on placement on the hearth, may be done before others. Remove the ones that are done, replace the others, and reseal the door. When perfectly baked, the loaves will be crusty, reddish brown, and shiny, and will resound with a hollow "thunk" when thumped with the fingertips.

PIZZA, PITA, AND FISH

Wood, fire, and brick make pizza a different food. That subtle smokiness, the light, crunchy crust, and the intensity of cooking made possible by the fire burning in the oven as the pizza cooks create flavors and textures unlike anything from either your kitchen range or the local pizzeria. Heating the oven for just one pizza is hard to justify, but what better focus for a party than the world's best pizza and the glowing warmth of the oven on a cool evening in the fading twilight?

Begin firing as for baking bread. When the bricks are burned clean, push the fire against the back of the oven, and toward one corner. Sweep the rest of the hearth with the wet broom. Keep the fire gently burning by tossing on an occasional split or two of wood. The oven air should be hot—over 600°F. The door remains open and the fire burning while the pizza bakes.

Place the flattened round of proofed dough on a flour- or cornmeal-dusted peel, assemble toppings, and place pizza directly on the hearth to bake. Once the crust has set, you can rotate the pizza for even cooking. If your oven is hot enough pizza will cook quickly—in as little as ten minutes. Experience will teach you. If you're making a number of pizzas you may have to move the fire around to keep the hearth hot.

Pita, those flat rounds with the pocket, are traditionally baked on the hearth of a very hot oven. I often bake a few at the end of a regular oven firing, after the fire has subsided, but before raking out the coals. Just push the fire aside, sweep that portion of the hearth clean, and place the unbaked rounds on the hearth with your peel. In moments, they'll puff up like pillows. Take them out before they turn crisp. If you want to make a lot of these, fire as for pizza.

Fish requires only a small fire and very little preheating. Build the fire in the back center of the oven using a wood with pleasantly aromatic smoke like alder, oak, fruitwood, or hickory. When the fire has started to burn down, push it toward one of the back corners and place a baking sheet with the prepared whole fish near the fire. You'll have to rotate the sheet a couple of times and maybe turn the fish over once during cooking. Especially delicious for us was a freshly caught local salmon, liberally rubbed inside with crushed garlic, olive oil, and white miso, with several sprigs of fresh garden basil in the cavity. Cooked until tender and flaky, the fish was moist and flavorful with a subtle blend of herbs and alder smoke. The fish, a salad of garden greens, an ear of local corn: probably the epitome of the emerging cuisine of fresh, regional ingredients, simple preparation, and innovative approaches to cooking.

USING THE OVEN EFFICIENTLY

Even though Alan Scott's modern, insulated brick ovens are considerably more efficient than their traditional forebears, careful planning can maximize use of the energy released in burning your wood. With no additional firing, the inside surfaces of the Lunde's oven are still hot to the touch and the air temperature over 275°F 24 hours after the firing. On the third day after a firing the chamber is still well above ambient outside temperature.

One fuel-saving strategy is to fire the oven again before it cools completely. It's surprising how little wood it takes to raise a small oven's temperature from 200° to 600°F compared with heating a cold oven to the same temperature. You may want to make pizza for a neighborhood party on Tuesday evening, re-fire lightly and bake the week's bread Wednesday afternoon, and cook a whole salmon when company comes for dinner on Thursday. When the fish is out, close the door, and just before retiring that night, pour boiling water over whole oats in a clay or enameled pot, cover, and slide into the oven for overnight simmering. Morning will bring forth a steaming pot of creamy porridge, ready for chopped nuts, fruit, and soymilk.

Alan suggests even more efficient use of the oven's heat: Start by making pita while the oven is being fired, follow that with a pizza or two, clean the oven, bake two batches of bread, followed by cake, pie, and cookies. Bake beans and grains overnight, use the oven for drying your kindling for the next firing, and finally for incubating yogurt as the temperature falls.

RESOURCES

Plans and Building Instructions for Three Brick Bread Ovens by brick-oven consultant and custom-designer Alan Scott can be had for $25 ppd. from **Oven Crafters**, Box 24, Tomales, CA 94971

Two masonry stove building companies that have also built commercial brick ovens are:
D. W. & S.
Box 323
Vashon, WA 98070

Masonry Stove Builders
R.R. 5
Shawville, Quebec J0X 2Y0 Canada

BIBLIOGRAPHY

Lise Boily and Jean-Francois Blanchette, *The Bread Ovens of Quebec*, National Museums of Canada, Ottawa, 1979.

Richard M. Bacon, *The Forgotten Art of Building and Using a Brick Bake Oven*, Yankee, Inc., Dublin, N.H., 1977.

John Downes, *The Natural Tucker Bread Book*, Hyland House Publishing Pty. Ltd., Melbourne, Australia, 1983.

Oliver Evans, *The Young Mill-Wright and Miller's Guide*, 13th Edition, Lea and Blanchard, Philadelphia, 1850.

Masanobu Fukuoka, *The One-Straw Revolution*, Rodale Press, Emmaus, Pa., 1978.

Sylvester Graham, *Bread and Bread Making*, Light and Stearns, Massachusetts, 1837. (Reprinted in 1970 by Provoker Press, St. Catherines, Ontario.)

Rudolph P. Hommel, *China at Work*, The John Day Company, New York, 1937. (Reprinted in 1969 by MIT Press, Cambridge, Mass.)

John Jeavons, *How to Grow More Vegetables*, Ecology Action, Palo Alto, Calif., 1974.

F. H. King, *Farmers of Forty Centuries*, Mrs. F. H. King, Madison, Wis., 1911. (Reprinted by Rodale Press, Emmaus, Pa.)

Gene Logsdon, *Small-Scale Grain Raising*, Rodale Press, Emmaus, Pa., 1977.

Laurel Robertson et al., *The Laurel's Kitchen Bread Book*, Random House, New York, 1984.

John Seymour, *The Guide to Self-Sufficiency*, Hearst Books, New York, 1976.

David Tresemer, *The Scythe Book*, Hand and Foot, Ltd., Brattleboro, Vt., 1981.

Alice Waters et al., *Chez Panisse Pasta, Pizza, and Calzone*, Random House, New York, 1984.

AUTHOR'S BIO

Thom Leonard lives in Salina, Kansas, and makes bread from Turkey Red, a hard winter wheat. He has written for numerous magazines on subjects ranging from the quality of sea salt to the use of horses on modern farms. His experience with food includes founding the first miso production shop in North America and making tempeh, beer, vinegar, and other assorted fermented foods. He now grows grain for seed and food, and directs The Grain Exchange, an organization fostering small-scale grain growing and genetic conservation.